SEA SOLDIERS OF PORTSMOUTH

SEA SOLDIERS OF PORTSMOUTH

A PICTORIAL HISTORY OF THE ROYAL MARINES AT EASTNEY AND FORT CUMBERLAND

JOHN AMBLER & MATTHEW LITTLE

In association with the Royal Marines Museum
Registered Charity Number: 259422

HALSGROVE

First published in Great Britain in 2008

British Library Cataloguing-in-Publication Data
A CIP record for this title is available from the British Library

ISBN 978 1 84114 743 7

HALSGROVE
Halsgrove House
Ryelands Industrial Estate, Bagley Road,
Wellington, Somerset TA21 9PZ
Tel: 01823 653777
Fax: 01823 216796
email: sales@halsgrove.com
website: www.halsgrove.com

Printed and bound in Great Britain by
CPI Anthony Rowe, Chippenham, Wiltshire

Contents

Royal Marine Artillery Sergeant, 1880.

Preface

SEA SOLDIERS of Portsmouth – A pictorial history of the Royal Marines at Eastney and Fort Cumberland describes and illustrates the long association between the Marines and their first and only purpose-built barracks in Portsmouth at Eastney, and the neighbouring land and fortification of Fort Cumberland. It focuses on the period from 1859, when the Royal Marine Artillery set up their divisional headquarters in the fort, to 1991 when the last Royal Marines units marched out of Eastney Barracks. Between those dates, the Royal Marines, the town of Portsmouth, the technology of conflict, and the expansion and contraction of the country's empire, changed dramatically.

The first company of Marines was billeted in Portsmouth in 1667 – about a hundred men. By 2008 the remaining Royal Marines Portsmouth Band (The Royal Band), The Royal Marines School of Music, and the headquarters staff on Whale Island, amount to barely double that. Portsmouth Division of Royal Marines moved from Clarence Barracks in old Portsmouth, to Forton in Gosport in 1848. Whilst the two converted barracks which once housed the Royal Marine Artillery of the town at 'Gun-Wharf' now lie under the prestigious commercial and residential development of the same name, the Georgian fort and Victorian barracks they moved east to, remain comparatively untouched.

With the Portsmouth Division reunited at Eastney in 1923 after the amalgamation of the Royal Marine Light Infantry ('Red Marines') and Artillery ('Blue Marines'), the barracks and surrounding area reached its peak of expansion and population up to 1947. Thereafter the demobilisation of HO (Hostilities Only) marines, the decline of Sea Service and Gunnery role, and contraction of the Corps into the new specialisation of amphibious and Commando warfare, eventually broke up the Royal Marines Divisional system that had existed since 1755.

Fort Cumberland was scheduled an ancient monument in 1964. It was taken into Guardianship when the Royal Marines left in the mid-1970s, and became the home to English Heritage's Centre for Archaeology. After continual reductions, Eastney was finally vacated by the Royal Marines in

1991, leaving the Royal Marines Museum in residence in the former Officer's Mess and quarters, and the remaining listed barracks to be internally converted into prestigious apartments.

Matthew Little
RM Museum 2008.

First Royal Marine Artillery helmet plate.

Acknowledgments

THE AUTHORS would like to thank the following for assisting with the production of this book:- The Trustees of the Royal Marines Museum, Eastney. Commander Brian Witts RN (Rtd) of the HMS *Excellent* Museum, Whale Island, Portsmouth. Paddy O'Hara, of English Heritage at Fort Cumberland. Nick Hall, Curator Royal Armouries Museum at Fort Nelson, Portsmouth and Ted Molyneux, Honorary Curator of the National Rifle Association Museum at Bisley. Also Margaret Ambler and Derek Gleed, two volunteers at the Royal Marines Museum.

We would also like to thank, in their absence, all those who took the photographs as well as those who donated them.

Helmet plate for Royal Marine Artillery blue cloth helmet.

Royal Marine Artillery Officer, 1816.

Introduction to the Pictures Collection

THE ROYAL MARINES Museum's Collections of paintings, drawings and photographs hold between two and three million images – a large number for a relatively small Corps. They are historical Collections, not picture libraries, and the Museum's objectives are to collect, preserve and make accessible, images that relate to any aspect of the history, including current events, of the Royal Marines.

Royal Marine Artillery Officer, 1912.

This publication is a welcome opportunity to make accessible images that illustrate a particular theme – in this instance the story of the impact that the Royal Marines, and in particular the Royal Marine Artillery, have had upon Eastney and the entire south-east part of Portsmouth. Both text and images have required a great deal of research and, particularly in the case of the images, careful selection and interpretation. We have not selected the images on artistic merit, we have selected them for the story they tell. Whether taken by professional photographer, by Official photographer or by a Marine using a Box Brownie on a dull, windswept evening in Eastney, matters not. These are the best examples of images, whether painting, photograph, map, plan or technical drawing, that illustrate particular aspects of the story that we have to tell. So, if you struggle with the quality of some of the images please bear in mind that you are actually looking at the best, possibly the only, image of that particular event, time or place. The wonders of modern technology do allow images to be 'digitally enhanced' but this will risk changing the content and meaning of the image. Some of the images in this publication have received some editing but only in a sympathetic manner. Brightness and contrast might have been adjusted and the picture itself could have been trimmed to eliminate damage to edges – but history has not been re-written, or altered in any way.

Readers might feel that there is a shortage of imagery relating to the past fifty years, the period that included the reductions to the Royal Marines' presence in the area, followed by the partial destruction and redevelopment of some of the sites. The reason for this is two-fold. Firstly we are using images that we hold in our own Collections and have resisted the temptation to do otherwise. Secondly, much of our photographic Collection is based upon material from Official sources, owned by the Crown and administered by the Ministry of Defence. As a result of the charges applied to images still under Crown copyright we, like many authors and publishers, try to avoid the additional cost to the reader by restricting coverage of this period to images from alternative sources.

We have taken the opportunity to increase our Collections and, hopefully, to improve your enjoyment of this publication, by taking additional photographs to further illustrate the subject. These show what places or buildings look like now, particularly where public access is restricted, as well as appropriate paintings and objects from Museum Collections.

Please enjoy this small selection of images from the huge Collection that I am privileged to administer and to curate – hopefully, other opportunities to bring you further selections will arise.

John Ambler
Photographs and Pictures Librarian
Royal Marines Museum 2008

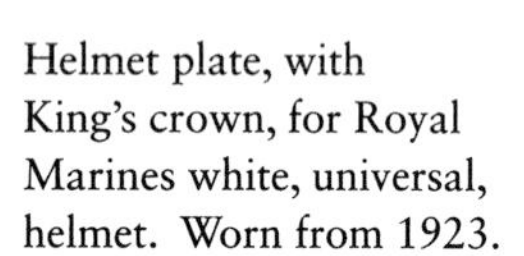
Helmet plate, with King's crown, for Royal Marines white, universal, helmet. Worn from 1923.

Introduction

On 28th October 1664 the Duke of York and Albany's Maritime Regiment of Foot, consisting of twelve hundred officers and men, was sanctioned by the Duke's brother, King Charles II. The formalisation of placing a specific regiment of soldiers aboard warships had begun, and in the process, so became the ancestors of the Royal Marines. By 5th November the officers had been commissioned, by the 16th the men had been mustered and paid, and by the 26th Sir Charles Lyttelton's Company was quartered at Southampton. Although raised due to the outbreak of the second Dutch War, when not afloat by design, it rarely operated in force. It occupied strategic fortresses such as Landguard Fort in Suffolk, which it was called upon to defend in July 1667, but ashore it generally maintained law and order in a half-hearted manner, and spent most of the time dispersed by companies, acting as a gendarmerie.

It was not until January 1667 that Captain Thomas Killigrew's Company were billeted at Portsmouth, and a look at maps of the town between 1600 and 1668 give an indication as to why. Portsmouth was a fortified walled town at the western point of Portsea Island at the mouth of the harbour. Apart from the King's stores houses (dockyard), Southsea Castle, Lumps and Eastney Farms, the rest of the island was mainly fields or marsh. With a garrison already in situ to man the defences, room for extra forces in a confined town was problematic.

With the Admiralty taking over the expense and administration of Marine forces in 1755, a permanent divisional system was introduced in each of the ports of Chatham, Portsmouth, and Plymouth numbered 1st, 2nd, and 3rd Divisions respectively. Portsmouth Division was formed on the 3rd April 1755, but had to wait a further ten years until a barracks could be provided in the town: a converted Cooperage and Brewery originally dating from 1613. This first barracks for the Marines of Portsmouth was named Clarence Barracks and was occupied on 20th May 1765, but not completed until 1769 with further extensions in 1828.

With the American, French Revolutionary and Napoleonic Wars escalating between 1775 and 1815, the size and expansion of Portsmouth Division put this barracks and the necessary outside billets under severe strain. A weekly return for the Division on 8th November 1799 placed the numerical establishment at eight thousand, one hundred and four officers and men. Fortunately, around six thousand, five hundred of them were at sea, or otherwise away from barracks, recruiting or sick. Even so, two thousand men in a small bastioned town put space at a premium.

Eventually, the Admiralty exchanged Clarence Barracks with the War Department's Forton Barracks in Gosport in 1848, and while Portsmouth Division moved its Royal Marines across the harbour for the next seventy-five years, the Royal Marine Artillery Companies that were attached to it from 1804, remained to occupy the 'Four House' barracks adjacent to the vacated Clarence Barracks. In 1837, having out-grown this adapted housing, they moved to the converted victualling stores at Gun-Wharf. As the Royal Marine Artillery began to specialise in land as well as sea gunnery, this accommodation provided no suitable practise area. The continual marching across the width of Portsea Island to exercise at Fort Cumberland and the small coastal batteries at Lumps Farm and Eastney convinced the Admiralty to exchange Gun-Wharf for the Fort in 1858. Henceforth the Royal Marine Artillery became instrumental in the development of the south eastern end, of what would become the City of Portsmouth.

1 The Royal Marine Artillery

GUNNERY IN ships of the Royal Navy during the age of sail had not changed significantly since the beginning of the eighteenth century. Its over-riding principle was a means to engage enemy ships of a similar design in sea combat, and the quest for advantage lay in the development of weapons of increasing range or weight of shot. The ideal outcome of such combat was to compel the enemy to surrender, rather than destroy the vessel, as lucrative amounts of prize money would be paid for a captured ship, its cargo and fittings. For this purpose, solid round shot was the ammunition of choice; it was simple to use, and had great disabling power in either dismasting or de-rigging and could dismount guns from their carriages. However, when it came to engaging permanent shore batteries or fortifications, the use of the "bomb vessel" was preferable. These vessels had served with the fleet since 1686 and were strongly built trading vessels of shallow draft, carrying 13 inch and 10 inch mortars and light guns – after 1779 carronades, for dealing with other surface vessels.

They had one quality not shared with larger ships; they fired shells. These had been tried in ship actions but had been discarded by conventional ships of the line on account of their low powers of penetration and the explosive danger to the ship carrying them. However, throwing a large fused shell at a high trajectory over earthworks or stone fortifications to explode in a plunging descent could be devastating to the heart or workings of the target, with the bonus of scattering shrapnel amongst its unfortunate occupants. This latter effect was achieved in ship-to-ship actions with conventional round shot sending wood splinters upon impact; hence the Navy had no real interest in the technology of mortars and their shells.

The Royal Navy therefore borrowed officers and Gunners from the Royal Artillery to man these vessels, providing simply a sailing crew for navigating the ship. Service in the "bomb vessels" was popular among young Gunners, as the Board of Ordnance, as masters of the Royal Artillery, made special concessions in the way of pay and service to officers and men thus employed.

The Navy itself seemed content to leave mortars alone, and made no attempt to form a Corps of Marine Artillery, although Colonel Campbell Dalrymple in a collection of "Military Essays," published in 1761, made the following suggestion for the formation of such a Corps: —

'Of all the various branches of our profession,' he wrote, ' none hath made a greater progress in it than the Regiment of Artillery...suppose, therefore, a Marine Battalion should be formed to serve aboard the Fleet, instead of what they call Quarter-Gunners, who, having no education or instruction till they are pressed and carried on board the Ships of War, are by no means equal to these men, regularly trained to the use of great guns, and from practice become excellent marksmen.'

In 1780, during the American War of Independence, a Marine Artillery Company was actually formed in New York but it is not known if it ever served afloat.

The problem that arose to threaten and eventually destroy this arrangement was a bureaucratic one involving Army personnel coming under the Naval Discipline Act. Occurrences began to arise of whether the naval commander of the bomb-vessel could order the officers and men of the Royal Artillery to take watch, as would be the case with an entirely "naval" complement (Marines included). Conversely in order to affect his ordnance, could the RA Officer order the naval officer to position his ship?

The uncertainty led to charges and counter-charges contesting the legality of discipline, and eventually after one such occurrence happening under Lord Nelson's command, the Admiralty sought their own solution – replace the Royal Artillerymen with a force already under the Naval Discipline Act: The Royal Marines.

The Royal Marine Artillery (RMA) was formed by Admiralty Order-in Council of the 18th August, 1804, after an exchange of correspondence between Lord Melville, the First Lord of the Admiralty, and Lord Nelson. By August 24th Commandants of Divisions were instructed to form RMA Companies, attaching one each to their divisions. A fourth company was added in 1805, when the new Woolwich Division of Royal Marines was created. Apart from providing crews for the mortars afloat, they were charged with drilling the whole of the Marines in gunnery, and hence scrounged what land artillery it could from the Board of Ordnance. Initially this comprised of an 18 pdr fortress gun, a 3 inch howitzer and two 6 pdr field guns, with six 6 pdr guns and two 5 inch howitzers being added later. Some 10 inch mortars were also found so that bomb vessel practise could take place ashore. After initial training from the Royal Artillery, the influence of this Corps resulted in the RMA becoming proficient in field guns and howitzers, shells and other types of shot and charge, and eventually even rockets. Augmented with their sea-service training, they were also able to fashion small vessels such as mortar boats, gun boats and rocket boats. The Royal Artillery would come to nick-name the RMA as "The Fish Gunners".

The officers were specially chosen from those having the necessary mathematical qualifications, while the NCOs and men were selected from those fitter and larger amongst each division. The Napoleonic War restricted the RMA from developing much of its home organisation, for once trained, detachments were immediately required for bomb vessel duty or overseas battalions and garrisons.

After gaining a reputation for usefulness afloat, an Admiralty minute in 1817 advocated their augmentation. It stated 'We are so well satisfied of the great utility of having a considerable body of marines trained to gunnery, that we are inclined to recommend that the Royal Marine Artillery be increased to eight companies, as well for the purpose of encouraging and training the other marines, as to enable us to embark a certain number of well trained artillerymen in others of his majesty's ships as well as in the bombs, experience having proved the great advantage to be derived to the service from this practice, which has been tried of late to a small extent'.

The headquarters of the Royal Marine Artillery since formation had been at Chatham Division. The expansion of 1817 caused Colonel Sir Richard Williams RMA to request a move to Portsmouth due to the heavy gun facilities not being adequate at Chatham. They were allocated Fort Monckton on the Stokes Bay side of Portsmouth Harbour and began to move in from 21st March. Here they used the 36, 24 and 18 pounder cannons for naval gun drill, and built a sea service mortar battery for training.

In 1822 Colonel Williams began to try to concentrate the RMA Companies at Portsmouth, or at least for their training. The "new" victualling store at Gun-Wharf was converted for the men's barracks while the officers were housed at No.110 High Street. In August, the RMA were sent as a temporary measure to the Upper Barracks, at Chatham, in consequence of 'the fever and ague having broken out to a great extent in the Corps, attended by glandular affection, &c., at Fort Monckton'. The Headquarters returned to Portsmouth in 1824.

By 1823 the Colonel had managed to secure the use of the guns of Southsea Castle, Fort Cumberland, Eastney and Lumps Forts for practise. Sea service mortars in drill batteries were erected at the Fire Barn – a large brick Ordnance building situated between Southsea and Eastney which also accommodated the 6 pdrs and field howitzers previously mentioned. In addition, one of the small shore batteries on the coast of Southsea Common was reconstructed and equipped to represent the gun-deck of a ship of the line, similar to the one built four years earlier while at Fort Monckton, except pierced for sea cannons.

In 1828, after the expansion of Clarence Barracks for Portsmouth Division, a block of adjacent buildings were used by the RMA, known as 'Four House Barracks'. Part of a rhyme at the time stated:-

'...Near this, with all accommodation
Befitting military station
Stand Four House Barracks – but for me,
I never yet found more than three.'

About this time the Admiralty began to look at its gunnery training and realised that the Royal Marines, and in particular the Royal Marine Artillery, were better skilled at gunnery than their own seamen. Whilst the Royal

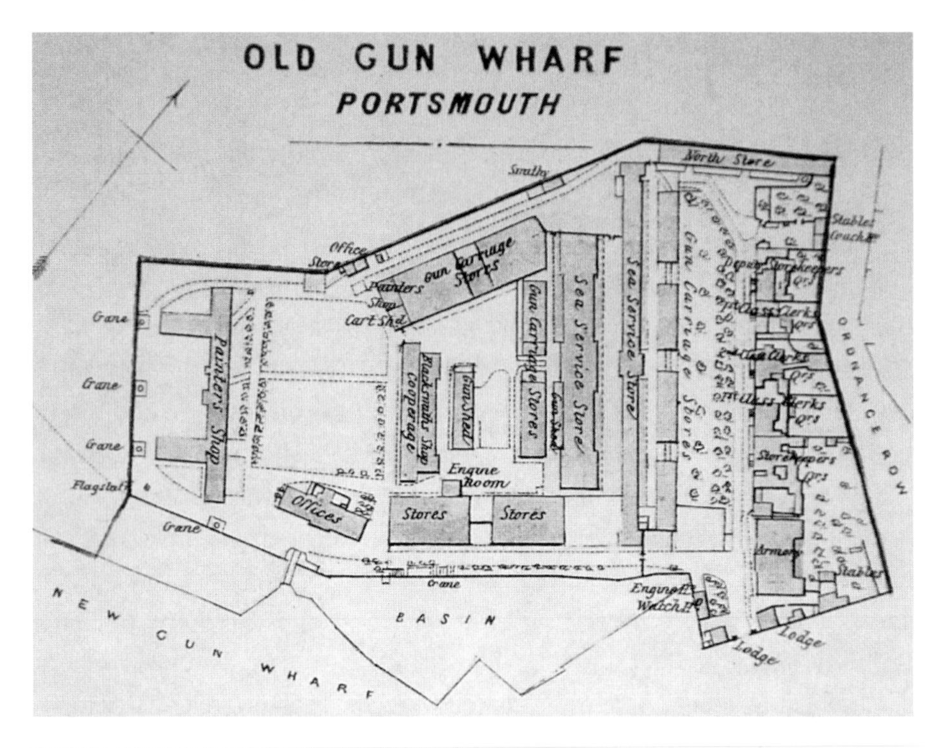

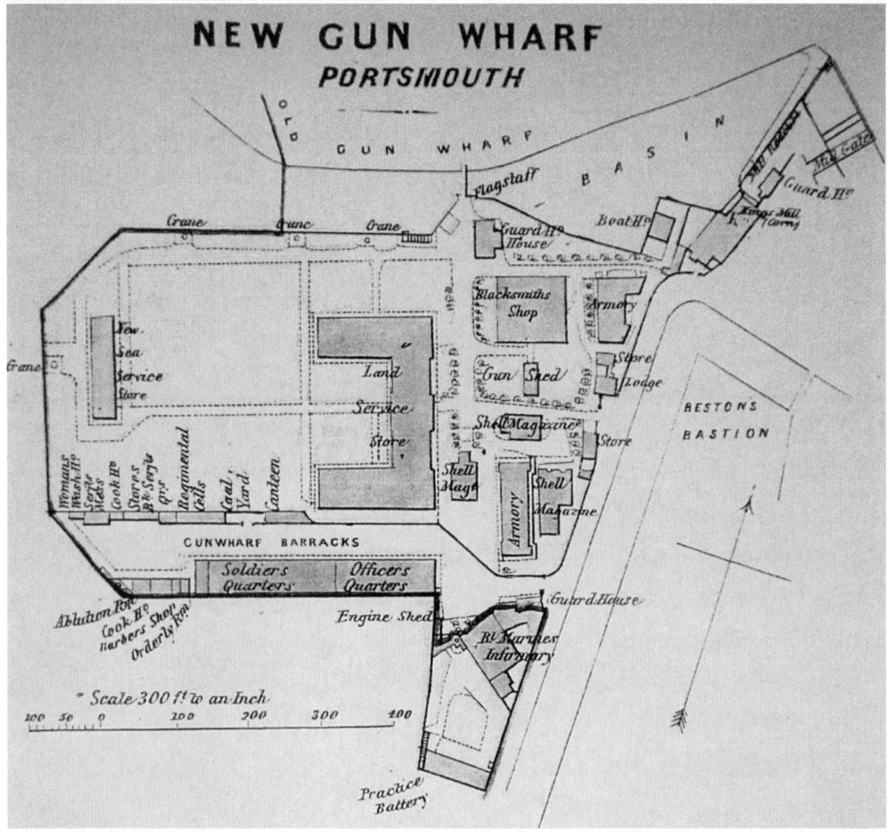

1859 Plans of 'Old' and 'New' Gun-Wharf, Portsmouth with the Royal Marines Barracks, Infirmary and practise battery marked. The RMA occupied buildings at the Wharf between 1822 and 1848.

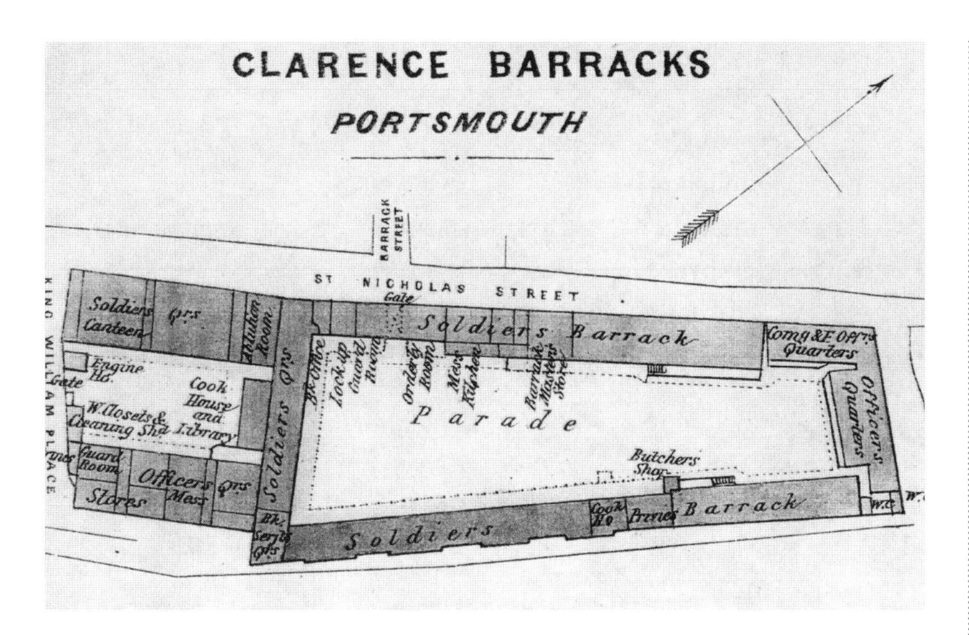

A plan of Clarence Barracks dated 1859.

Marines had established continuous voluntary service since 1755, the Navy still press ganged its seamen, and paid them off at the end of a ship's commission. Any skills and experience gained was instantly disposed of, and had to be re-started with whatever 'recruits' they mustered for the next commission. The simple round shot, smooth bore naval gun was also destined to become obsolete, and the more technical weapons that were being developed could stretch the capabilities of their raw material if training was not addressed. So in 1830 the Naval School of Gunnery was started aboard *HMS Excellent*, moored near Fareham Creek.

It was at first flattering for the RMA to have Lieutenants Dover Farrant, Thomas Holloway, and John Harvey Stevens amongst the instructor staff in the initial years. Along with senior NCOs and Gunners, who had worked at the laboratory in the Fire-barn, they were appointed for the theoretical instruction of naval officers and seamen gunners, and also to instruct them in the laboratory works required for the naval service. This work included

Originally built as the King's Cooperage and Brewery in 1613, these buildings were converted into a barracks for Portsmouth Division of Marines. This watercolour depicts the barrack square sometime around 1805 if the uniforms are accurate.

Clarence Barracks depicted after the clock had been installed above the officers' quarters in 1842.

such activities as making rockets for signals, filling tubes, priming them, and filling cartridges, etc.

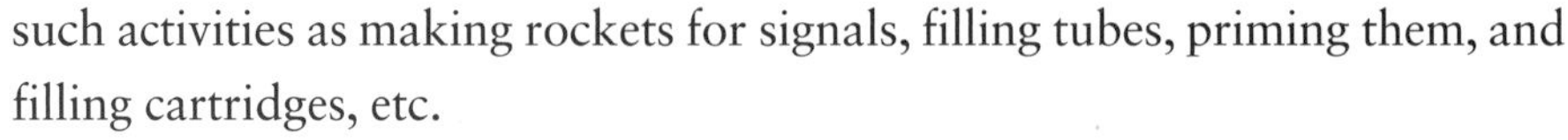

By 1832 the Royal Navy had also come to recognise that the exploding shell was going to replace the solid shot. This was the swan song for mortar boats for the time being and, on the adoption of shells for all vessels of the Fleet, all bomb vessels were scrapped except two—HMS *Erebus* and HMS *Terror* which found fame and oblivion in Franklin's polar expedition. Without the bomb vessels, the RMA had lost a main sea role, and with them now training the Navy in the use of shells, their continued existence was called into question. Sir James Graham, as First Sea Lord, saw an opportunity for the Navy to gain its own expertise in gunnery and save money in the process. From this date the RMA was reduced to two companies with many of the redundant gunners and NCOs transferring to be Able Seaman and Petty Officers in the Royal Navy and forming the nucleus of the new gunnery school at HMS *Excellent*. Some others transferred out to the Royal Artillery.

Colonel George Digby CB RMA, who as a Captain, commanded a mortar boat flotilla at the bombardment of Sevastopol in 1855. He also pioneered the science of naval gunfire support by inventing the "Digby Laying Calculator" intended to 'enhance the accuracy of plunging fire in the overcoming of fortresses by seaborne guns'.

With some irony, Lieutenant T S Beauchant RMA published *The Naval Gunner* in 1835, tabling and listing all the gunnery skills to that day. It was one of the first 'modern' gunnery handbooks. Two other characters maintained the Royal Marines connections with HMS *Excellent* as the school developed; Colour-Sergeant J Mullins RMA, and former Sergeant Major Bacon RMLI. The former served amongst the instructor staff and was later resident, with his wife, on Borrow Island, sometimes known as Rat Island off Royal Clarence Yard. The island was used as a target bearing and also a depot for moored targets. However, as the Navy would construct unmanned facilities, so they would be plundered by the so called 'Landport Pirates' who would row out to acquire anything of value. Hence a house was built on the island in 1861 and Mr Mullins served as the resident security, although on one occasion a sudden loud training salvo deafened his mother–in-law and killed the pet canary. After his Royal Marine service with 6th Company RMA and his time on Rat Island, he was awarded a Long Service & Good Conduct Medal in 1868. Sergeant-Major Bacon RMLI, on the other hand became manager of the men's Canteen at HMS *Excellent* from 1883 to 1898 where the turnover under his tenancy started at £6200 a year.

General Francis Edward Halliday RMA. After serving aboard bomb vessels at the bombardment of Sweaborg in 1855, he went on to become Commandant at Eastney in 1886. He was the cousin of General Sir Lewis Halliday RMLI who won the Victoria Cross at Peking in 1900.

Having criticised the First Sea Lord's decision as "suicidal" Colonel Williams retreated with his two remaining companies to Fort Cumberland where they were allocated a casement. From here over the next two years one company would be at sea whilst the other remained ashore training. After service in Portugal in 1836 the RMA moved to the 'old' victualling store at Gun-Wharf in 1837, before joining Lord Hay's squadron in operations in the Spanish Carlist War of 1837-40.

The transition from sail to steam and the continued pace of development of gunnery and eventually armour in the Navy has been said to have encouraged the Admiralty to rebuild the RMA during the 1840s and 1850s. The hasty decision to scrap the bomb vessels was regretted when the Crimean War (1854-56) required shallow draught vessels to deliver bombardments of fortifications at short range; smaller mortar and rocket boats were once more manned by the RMA reviving their old skills. The RMA were back to a strength of one thousand, seven hundred and twenty officers and men by the start of the war. It was perhaps fitting that the two Victoria Crosses won by the RMA in the conflict were awarded for gallantry on land service for Gunner Thomas Wilkinson, and sea service for Lieutenant George Dare Dowell RMA.

General Sir Charles Menzies KH who was appointed the first Colonel of the Royal Marine Artillery Division on 28th March 1863.

The RMA became a separate division and took up residence in Fort Cumberland on 2nd November 1858. Just over a year later Colonel John Fraser became the first "Commandant" of the division there, on 21st November 1859.

2 **Fort Cumberland**

THE MILITARY significance of Eastney Point on the eastern extremity of Portsea Island had been recognised in the early eighteenth century, and an earthwork battery was built on the point to defend the entrance to Langstone Harbour in 1716.

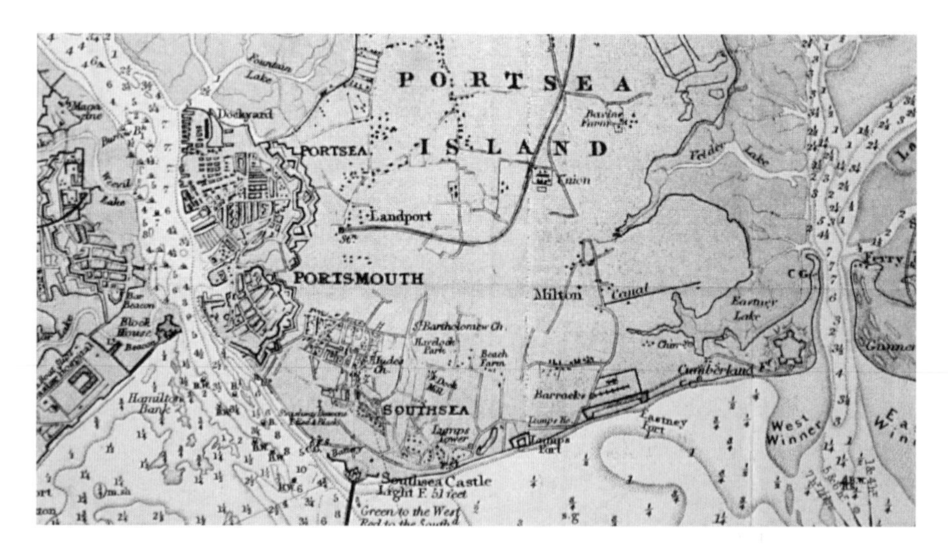

Map of Portsea Island showing the first Fort Cumberland with the second fort superimposed, the two Eastney Forts and the main Barrack Block at Eastney. c. 1868.

The Jacobite Rebellion of 1745, with the claim of Charles Stuart for the throne of England, posed an increased threat of a French invasion to support their Scottish allies. Following the defeat of the Stuart prince and his supporting army of Highland Clansmen at Culloden in 1746, the Duke of Cumberland was made the Cabinet's Military Advisor by his father, George II.

He reviewed the nation's defences, and as a result, designs for a new fort on Eastney Point were submitted by the Ordnance Engineer John Desmaretz.

The construction of a star-shaped fort of earth with rubble stone revertments was begun in 1747, based around, it is believed, a farm house used by the Duke as a shooting lodge on a slight rise called Monkey Island. The projecting points of the star allowed defensive fire in all directions, and this idea was expanded when it was decided to rebuild the fort some forty years later. Charles Lennox, the Duke of Richmond, was made Master of the Ordnance and with deteriorating political relations with France following the War of American Independence, his review of Portsmouth's defences recommended a pentagonal fort with projecting defensive earthworks (bastions) at the end of each length of curtain wall. Built of brick and Portland limestone, it was the last bastion-traced fort to be constructed, and represents the pinnacle of this design form. Two of the buildings from the first fort were retained and reused – the Guardhouse and the Storehouse.

This second Fort Cumberland was improved with vaulted casemates within the curtain wall. Its low lying profile presented a difficult target for the trajectory of direct fire ships' cannon or landed field pieces, but defensive forts could still be vulnerable to the plunging explosive shells of howitzers and mortars. To counter this, free-standing buildings were kept to a minimum and the stores, men and powder magazines were moved to the relative safety of the curtain wall. Gravel was used to infill the brick arches that would dissipate any shell charge, protecting those housed beneath.

Materials had begun to be delivered to the site in 1783, but shortages and the time taken to transport stone and brick, necessitated brickworks and kilns to be set up so that the estimated five million bricks could be produced on site. The labour was a mixture of contract and convict, and the use of the unwilling element had slowed progress, not least for their daily four mile escorted march from the Portsmouth Harbour prison hulks. Once enough of the construction was secured, convicts were housed within the site. However in October 1810 they mutinied in a bid to escape, and the 8th Veteran Battalion employed as their guards managed to quell the riot before the arrival of elements of the town garrison and Royal Marines from Clarence Barracks. After this incident, the convicts were housed aboard hulks that were towed round to Langstone Harbour.

On completion in 1812, the fort was manned by a rotation of regiments forming the Army garrison of Portsmouth, with the ordnance manned by a detachment of Royal Artillery.

It was not until June 1817 that four RMA companies were deployed to the fort for further exercises. This occurred once the RMA had expanded to eight companies and transferred their training to Fort Monckton on the Gosport side of Portsmouth Harbour. The Admiralty had come to an arrangement with the Commander-in-Chief of the Army for the RMA to practise at the various Royal Artillery batteries at Portsmouth, and this was further enhanced when in June 1823, a detachment of RMA took up quarters at Fort Cumberland. The fort was garrisoned at this time by the 53rd Foot (Shropshire Regiment) and thereafter

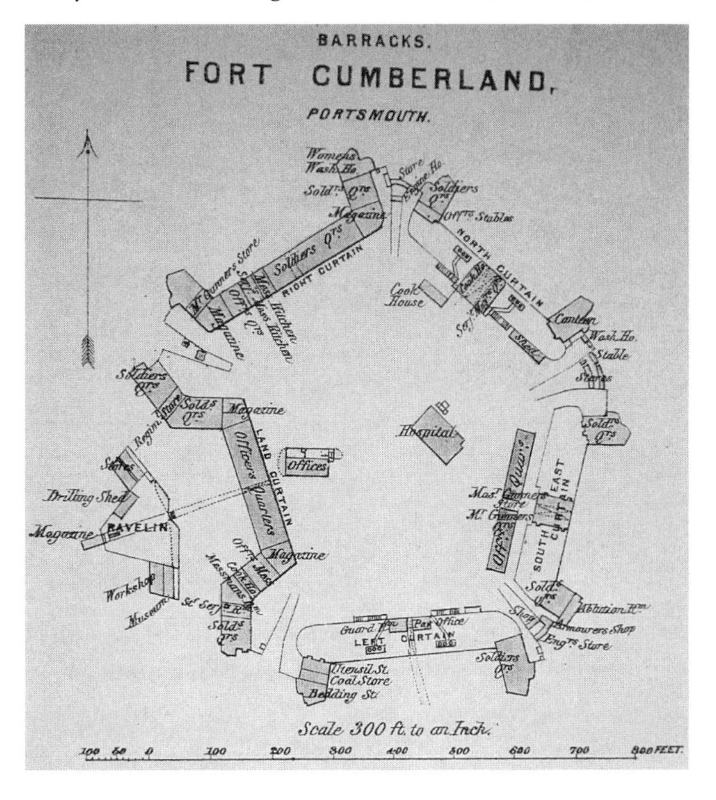

Plan of the buildings contained within the fortifications of Fort Cumberland c.1859.

arrangements were made to recondition the entire fort as a gunnery establishment. The ravelin and magazines were prepared for taking stores and ammunition, and the construction begun of mortar and ship-gun platforms and of ranges and butts on the Ordnance waste ground adjacent. A broadside battery was constructed in the North-East bastion, and a pivot battery near the South Gate. There was also a 'sea-service' battery constructed at Langstone Point, and called Point Battery, which was originally armed with two 32 pdr smooth-bore cannons, with the old convicts' mortuary being used as the Officer Instructor's office. Later, these weapons were replaced with two Armstrong guns that arrived from Woolwich by sea on 10th March 1860; the other guns of this shipment sailed on to be mounted at the gunnery school at HMS *Excellent* in Portsmouth harbour. The battery would be demolished between 1876-7.

Convict labour was largely utilized once again with the gangs being marched out daily from the former third rate HMS *York*, now a convict hulk in Portsmouth Harbour. Portsmouth dockyard authorities furnished the materials for the platforms and traversing tables, from stores of old ship timbers, while the RMA supervised the construction. One such training piece was a 6 pdr smooth-bore mounted on a platform, which by turning a winch wheel was made to represent a ship rolling. Recruits fired solid shot at a target 600 yards distant and quite close to the fort. The shot was then recovered from the target sand butt.

The Royal Marine Artillery was inspected at Fort Cumberland on three notable occasions within the next twenty years. Firstly in 1827 HRH the Duke of Clarence, the Lord High Admiral, witnessed gun and mortar practice, and then "inspected a new method of disembarking heavy pieces of ordnance, when the surf is so great on a beach that no boat can ground the beach to do it. A line was thrown ashore from the boat, to which the gun was lashed, by a small mortar. The gun was then disengaged from the boat, and the party to whom the line had been conveyed drew it to the shore. Afterwards, the gun carriage was sent ashore in a similar way and the gun re-fixed to the carriage and fired. The whole service was affected in fourteen and a half minutes. At this inspection a model of a revolving mortar was laid before His Royal Highness by Bombardier Alexander Wilson, it being designed to save the manual labour in traversing, etc. It is totally unconnected with either wheels screws or springs. His Royal Highness expressed himself highly gratified and greatly admired the workmanship, which was all 'turned,' the principal part for revolving being entirely hid from observation."

Secondly, Major-General Sir James Cockburn, visiting the fort in 1835, 'witnessed the firing of rockets...when the floating target, at a distance of 900 yards, was completely riddled', and shell fire at the same distance 'burst with beautiful effect and precision, just as it reached the destined spot'.

Thirdly in 1844, in a similar exercise for Lord Auckland and the Board of Admiralty, the Royal Marine Artillery under the command of Colonel D

Anderson Gibsone, demonstrated an 8 inch howitzer and a 12 pdr medium gun destroying a floating target at 900 yards, whilst a 32 pdr sea-service gun sent shells accurately 1500 yards. Also displayed with praiseworthy accuracy, were three 10 inch land service mortars, several 68 pdrs, some 32 pdr carronades, a wide selection of Congreve rockets and four 6 pdrs. His Lordship could only express 'the high gratification he had experienced at the most excellent practice he had that day witnessed'.

The training on such a diversity of weapons served the RMA companies well in the Carlist War in Spain in 1837, and later in the Crimean War 1854-56. The companies attached to Portsmouth Division that then deployed to operations in the Indian Mutiny and the second China War in 1857 and 1858, returned home to find they had become a separate division in their absence.

On the formation of the Artillery division, the Admiralty exchanged Gun-Wharf Barracks for Fort Cumberland in 1858, with headquarters formally taking residence on the 2nd November. Lieutenant Duncan Pitcher RMA wrote at the time that they 'marched in full dress uniform out of Gun-Wharf and across to the fort, where the bitterly severe winter, 1858-9, was spent'.

General Edmund Henry Cox RMA, who had extensive service during the Crimean war of 1854-56 before his arrival at Fort Cumberland. He died in 1893 and is buried in Highland Road Cemetery, Southsea, near to Eastney Barracks.

Under an Army occupation return of this date, the fort held twenty three officers and seven hundred and one men, but shortly after the RMA took over the official return showed only half this number. The former lodge cum guard-house of 1747 became the Commandant's, Adjutant's and Paymaster's offices, Orderly Room and Junior NCOs' library, and later, the Repository lecture rooms. The officers were placed in Nos. 1-5 casements in the land curtain until their new quarters were completed. When finished these had a billiard room at the north end, and the Quartermaster's store at the south end. It is said that these officers' quarters were converted from those used by the officers of the 8th Veteran Battalion guarding the original convicts. A plan published in 1859 shows the two blocks in existence, to which a cookhouse was added in 1860. The bricks for these buildings were made from clay from the Glory Hole. From about 1882 to 1890 the room built as a Quartermaster's store was used as a classroom for the probational 2nd

What appear to be 60ft shear legs (18metres) together with a capstan are being used to move and raise a gun-barrel. In the background can be seen the waters of Eastney Lake and the tall buildings and chimneys of the original Sewerage Pumping Station.

Lieutenants RMLI, who underwent their military course there. The Military Instructor lived in the house next door.

The fort was drained and water laid on in 1859-60, prior to which the water supply consisted of a well in the centre of the parade, the water from which was rather brackish but considered "by no means unwholesome". This was closed in and lost sight of until a tractor wheel ran over it during the First World War. The cast iron pump that was placed outside the guard house as part of the improvements met a similar end in 1949 when a truck backed into it and consigned it to the scrap heap before anyone could be reminded of its age.

Rats infested the fort to such "annoying degree" as to warrant application being made for a rat-catcher.

With a gun barrel slung below a very large gun-carriage, gunners pull it along Ferry Road. Note the amount of shipping in Langstone Harbour and the curved structures that mark the ferry jetty on Hayling Island.

It was common for manned sea defences such as forts and batteries to coast watch and supplement the Coast Guard service, and if a ship was seen to be in difficulty for example, a warning gun would be fired as an alarm. A lifeboat house had been constructed at a cost of £250 on the south side of Hayling Island, and on 14 January 1865 the schooner *Ocean* was blown onto the Woolsiner Shoal during gale force winds. A warning gun was fired from Fort Cumberland and Major F W Festing RMA and a mixture of Gunners and local fishermen put to sea in a cutter, rescuing three of the crew and assisting the lifeboat before the schooner was wrecked. He was awarded a silver medal for his action – the lifeboat house later became the pub "The Inn on the Beach".

General Sir Francis Worgan Festing CB KCMG RMA, died whilst Commandant at Eastney in October 1886. His influence within the RMA and Portsmouth in general was to result in a Road, a Grove, and a Hotel being named after him. He is buried in Highland Road Cemetery in Southsea, and later a memorial plaque was placed in the new St Andrew's Church.

The other original 1747 building, the storehouse, was utilised as a School, the Infirmary and Infirmary Sergeants' quarters being added. In the course of time the school room was embodied in the infirmary and was used as such until a new infirmary was built in Eastney Fort East in the 1880s, after which it became the Land Service lecture room.

Apart from the billiard room, the officers had the fives court (ball court) outside the south gate, and an eight-oared boat in which they did a great deal of rowing. A nine-hole golf course was built on the glacis of the fort in 1890, the greens of which were never very good, but it continued to be played on till about 1902-3. A theatre was started in the fort in the 1860s, near the North-East bastion, with Captain F E Halliday RMA and Lieutenant S T

Bridford painting the scenery and managing the performances. The only other means of recreation for the men were a skittle alley lit by tallow candles, parallel bars, and quoits were played in the ditch, while the junior NCOs had a bagatelle table. At one period boxing too was very popular.

Lifting a heavy muzzle-loader gun barrel onto the walls of the Fort from the dry moat using only manpower. To the right a number of men turn a capstan winch whilst others use ropes to 'steer' the barrel along the substantial timber beams.

As with any location that was deemed 'old' by the men who found themselves posted there, rumours were rife that the fort was of course haunted. Gunner Patrick Mee wrote in the 1890s of having been told by the older soldiers of the ghost of a man who had completed many years exemplary service. This man at a kit inspection was found to have lost his button polishing stick, and was ordered to re-muster his kit the following day by the inspecting officer. Apparently having taken this minor reprimand to heart, the man hanged himself that night. Thereafter men on watch at No 2 post would report seeing a figure by the old pump near the gate of the fort, usually between midnight and two in the morning, laying out his kit as if to be inspected. Such was the superstition that men on this sentry duty were issued with a whistle to summon assistance if need be. On one occasion, suitably jittered, a sentry new to this post blasted his whistle in panic, and was found by the turned out guard to be challenging with a fixed bayonet, the chain tethered goat on the rampart next to a chimney pot of the lower casement. The wind that night had been producing a moaning noise across the pot, and the goat deployed on grass trimming duty had wrapped the chain round it and was dragging at it to unwind itself!

Typical Fort cumberland casement chimney, as referred to in the text.

In 1899 Major Aubrey Hamilton Cox RMA became Instructor of Gunnery at the fort, which by now, as a gunnery establishment, was having its heyday. The main purpose of the fort from the RMA perspective had been a training area for gunnery, but also repository drill – disassembling and assembling artillery pieces and moving them ashore by gyns and beams, or by creating piers and bridges. The fort afforded a suitable mixture of terrain to affect this training and simulate battlefield situations. Guns could be

Land Artillery a) The use of Land Artillery was as important as ships gunnery to the men of the RMA. Fort Cumberland easily provided space within its fortifications for the men to practice bringing their guns into action. b) The shoreline outside the fort provided the opportunity to practice bringing their guns ashore. This scene, showing gun limbers being run ashore from whalers, is reminiscent of the Royal Tournament's famous Field Gun Run. c) Such activity required the men of the RMA to have seamanship skills – including boat handling. Here the skills of rowing are being practiced. The Lord Commissioners of the Admiralty periodically visited Eastney to inspect the RMA. Here, d) during the inspection of 3rd June 1901, they can be seen in discussion with senior officers and e) watching the men at repository drill. This picture also shows the scale of the defence works of Fort Cumberland and, together with the adjacent coast, deep water and open ground, why Eastney was such an effective training area for the RMA. f) Live firing was also part of the inspection as seen in this photograph (c.1907) of 4.7 inch siege guns on the ranges. Finally, at g), the RMA Field Battery Class of December 1919 pose, with the guns, inside the fort.

A party of Gunners altering the elevation of a mortar using a number of levers to move the heavy barrel. 1900.

pulled and swung across the dry moats and ditches for example, field construction of A-frames and rope bridges (across the ditch), as well as the use of pontoons and rafts in the adjacent Langstone Harbour, or Eastney beach.

The Major did experience fire of another sort on 6th January 1902 when smoke was seen'… at the official residence of Major A. H. Cox, at Fort Cumberland. The cause — a very old one — a domestic drying her clothes before an unauthorized fire in her bedroom. Result — a good deal of damage to a couple of the bedrooms by fire and water. The NCOs and Gunner, residing at Fort Cumberland, were promptly on the spot, and extinguished the fire without extraneous assistance' (from the *Globe & Laurel* 1902).

The fort's defensive weaponry underwent a number of modifications as the technology of artillery developed. The significant advance came in 1854 when William Armstrong developed a system of rifling inside the gun barrel with a series of spiralling grooves. Forcing the shells to spin on being fired, improved both accuracy and range. Fortifications and ships began to mount Rifled-Muzzle-Loading (RML) and Rifled-Breech-Loading (RBL) guns, as did land artillery. The use of these weapons transformed the design of future defences and vessels, and the ranges they would engage, with the necessary counter measures of earthwork and armour respectively. This advance was to impact on the fort as well as the building of Eastney Forts East and West.

Fort Cumberland's Defensive Ordnance

1750	14 x 32 pounders	14 x 18 pounders	4 x 9 pounders	2 x 6 pounders
1810	17 x 24 pounders	51 x 18 pounders	29 x 12 pounders	7 x 6 pounders
1862	3 x 7" RBL	14 x 8" guns	28 x 32 pounders	

Although the RMA at the fort had exercised the weaponry since 1823, the defence of the fort was the responsibility of the Royal Artillery detachments quartered there.

In the 1890s the fort was equipped with 6 inch breech-loading hydropneumatic guns that sat on disappearing gun carriages enabling the guns to be protected within their concrete emplacements between firing rounds. In 1895 a High Angle Fire Battery (designed in response to the development of armour-clad warships) was added; one of only five other batteries constructed in this country. The guns were fired at a high angle (between 30° and 75°) so their shells plunged on to the vulnerable decks of the warships, bypassing the thick steel armour plating on the ships' sides. However, by the turn of the century the development of static coastal defence was slowing, not only to the more rapid technology of warship design such as *Dreadnought* type vessels, but also because of the expense of maintenance and updating.

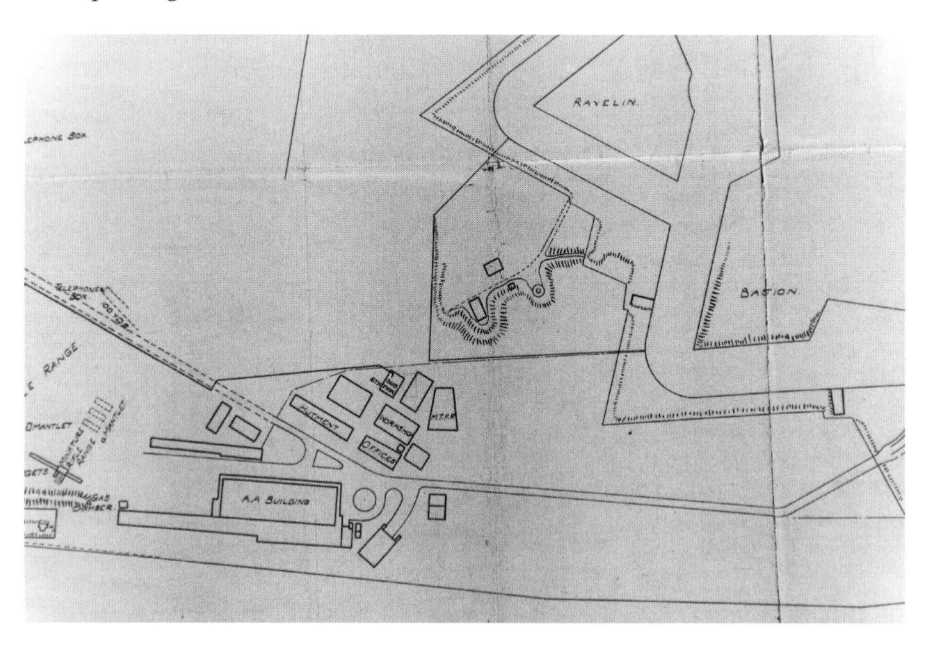

In the centre of this plan, which shows parts of Fort Cumberland (top right) and the Fraser Battery (bottom left), can be seen the emplacements for the High Angle Mortar Battery. Although much overgrown these important features are still visible.

The next era for the fort would follow on from the repository and training role, and see vehicles, landing craft, searchlights, motor cycles, machine and anti-tank guns being trained with.

Fort Cumberland was described by Nikolaus Pevsner in his influential *Buildings of England* book series of 1951-1974 as 'perhaps the most impressive piece of eighteenth-century defensive architecture in England'.

3 Building Eastney Barracks

THE AREA of Southsea towards Eastney was, until the early nineteenth century, mainly open fields, furze common and marsh, interspersed with random cottages, windmills and farms. On the coast there was a reference to Tudor batteries placed to defend the mouth of Langstone Harbour and south of Lumps Farm in 1539, prior to the building of Southsea Castle in 1544.

Pencil sketch of Proe's Farm drawn by Lt Cuthbert Suther RMA in 1859. It shows a cart to the right which was used by Miss Proe to transport the first Commandant, Colonel John Fraser RMA, daily to Fort Cumberland from the High Street in Old Portsmouth. The farm house was demolished in 1877.

The land that would become Eastney is first listed as a farm of 197 acres belonging to Mr Cotton in 1627. In 1716 the farm passed to James Osmond, trustee of the Order of the Baptists, a sect much persecuted at that time. Meetings were held at the farm with converts being baptized in a small pond. This pond was later part of Proe's Farm, named after a French refugee (then spelt Proux) of the Revolution, who had assisted in the service of the Duke of Kent and subsequently lived there rent free. Part of the acreage had been purchased by this time by the White family, with former Mayor of Portsmouth John White purchasing more in 1772. In 1817, on the death of Mary White, the land passed into the estate of Admiral Sir Phillip Charles Calderwood Henderson Durham and remained in his family until his death in Naples in 1845, when it was sold by his daughter Anne to the Crown for £15000.

By this time, the battery forts at Lumps Farm and Eastney had been rebuilt and re-armed during the Napoleonic War, but by the 1820s had fallen

Major General George Gardiner Alexander CB RMA first joined the RMA as 2nd Lieutenant in 1838 and went on to become Commandant of the RMA in 1865. After his retirement his expertise in Asiatic matters led to a request by the Foreign Office for him to take charge of the first Japanese Embassy in Britain.

into disrepair and obsolete redundancy. The substantially rebuilt Fort Cumberland had been completed in 1812 and was currently the main defensive fortification on the eastern side of Portsea Island.

When Napoleon III became Emperor of France in 1852, Britain became allied and the nations deployed their forces in 1854 against the Russians in the Crimean War. After the peace of 1856, political and diplomatic relations began to deteriorate as France began to aspire to an overseas empire once more. The nervousness in Britain resulted in a Royal Commission in 1859 to review the country's defences and manning against possible French invasion. Coastal fortifications and harbour defences received upgraded gunnery, and in many cases new construction. Much of the report focused on the channel coast, and ports such as Portsmouth in particular. Fort Cumberland and the existing defences of Portsmouth were to be improved, with the addition of an outer landward ring of brick forts from Bedhampton to Fareham to supplement those defending the north-west of Gosport. To this, a line of sea forts across the Solent was also recommended. The replacement of the abandoned Eastney Battery was included with two coastal emplacements at Eastney; Fort East and Fort West.

Drawings were received in December 1860 for the two forts and a connecting defensible parapet wall, and work was commenced in June 1861. They were intended to command the approach to Langstone Harbour and the water to the east of the proposed sea fort of Horse Sand. The face of each battery and of the connecting parapet was covered by a dry ditch and the gorge was closed by a loop-holed wall three feet thick. Each battery was constructed with ten embrasures and two guns en-barbette.

Although the RMA had now become a separate division with its headquarters in Fort Cumberland, it was still having to deploy some of its seventeen companies in places like Fort Monckton and Fort Elson in the early 1860s. By 1862 it had expanded to twenty-four, and the need for a new barracks for nearly three thousand men became paramount.

A copy from the original plan for Eastney Forts East and West in 1860, prior to barrack plans being submitted.

The 1859 Royal Commission had proposed a new barracks 'to occupy an empty section of shoreline further up the coast at Eastney', while the new forts were 'to form a defensible post for troops employed in opposing a landing'.

Many of the brick, casemated keeps of the Royal Commission forts, batteries and barracks built at this time, combined artillery works with secure, defensible garrison accommodation. However, as this logic was literally being cemented into bricks and mortar, Monsieur Stanislas Dupuy de Lone had designed and just launched the French warship *La Gloire*. This ocean-going iron-clad vessel, armed with thirty-six 163mm rifled muzzle loading guns not only rendered every Royal Navy ship obsolete overnight, it also would expose the susceptibility of static masonry defences to rifled gunfire. By August 1861 the British had commissioned the iron-hulled HMS *Warrior* in reply, yet this reaction was confined to ship versus ship; the programme for coastal defence remained unmodified at the time. These Royal Commission forts however, would be the last built in the country to amalgamate a defensive barracks with a battery emplacement.

The building of Eastney Forts East and West continued, and were completed in March 1863 for the sum of £17,435. Due to the uncertainty of the barrack build, the rear walls of both structures were pierced for heavy cannon in case of landward assault. Previously in October 1861, memorandums were still being exchanged between the Admiralty and the War Office finalising the exact location for the build of the new barracks. Whether by intention or interpretation, the two works that had certainly started life separately became one.

Eastney Barracks was to be the responsibility of the head of the Admiralty Works Department, Colonel Greene RE, and his civilian assistant, William Scamp, working in co-operation with Major William Drummond Jervois. Greene and Scamp were responsible for the contemporary extension of the Royal Marines Barracks at Stonehouse, Plymouth, as well as a number of important new buildings in the naval yards. Although many sources state the building of Eastney commencing in 1862, all the remaining drawings of the men's barracks, drill shed, and married quarters, in the Archives of the Royal Marines Museum, are dated between 1863 and 1868. A description of the time states:

'The Barracks will stand on an extensive piece of ground, and its front will have a long defensive work consisting of a long curtain (bank) with a heavy work at either end (Eastney Fort East and Fort West) in line with the

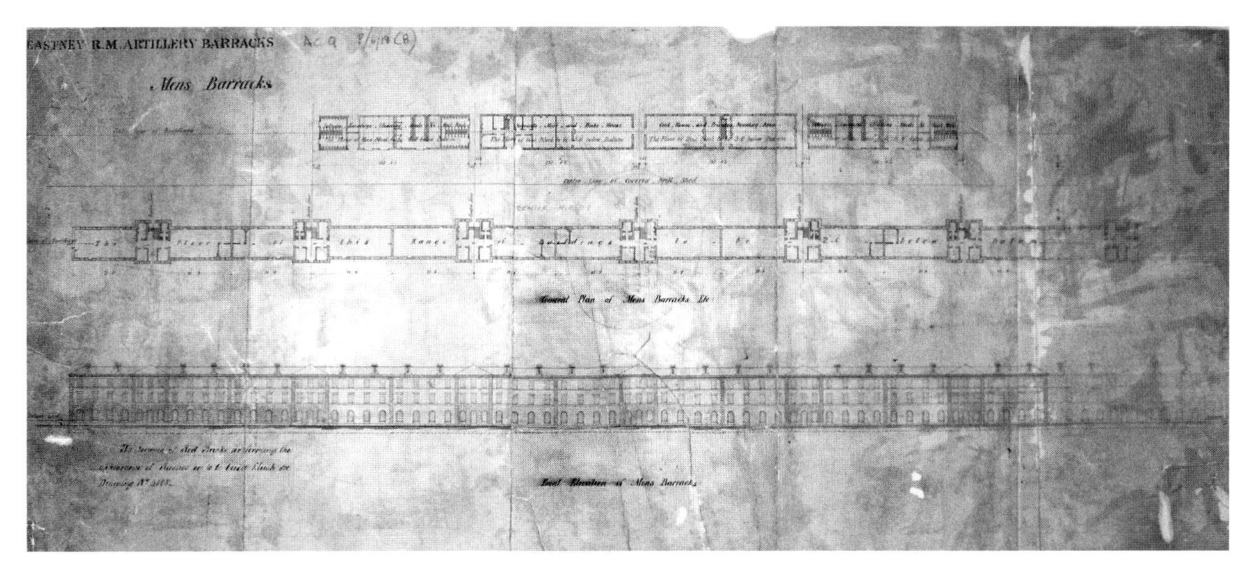

Original elevation and plan of the men's main barrack block, at Eastney.

Eastney Fort East a) Looking from the top of Eastney Fort East over the Museum car park to Eastney Fort West in the distance. The grass covered connecting defensive wall can be seen on the right. The last weapon to be sited in the caponier in the foreground was a 64pdr rifled muzzle loader. b) Through the gap between the connecting wall and the fort can be seen the men's barracks (Gunners' Walk). The end wall of the south wing of the Officers' Mess, now Royal Marines Museum, is on the right. c) The bastion for the 6 inch breach loading hydro-pneumatic (disappearing) gun in Eastney Fort East and, beyond, the Fire Commander's Station and Chart Room with, below it, the magazine. To the left can be seen the defensive flint wall bordering the track from the barracks to the Sea Service Battery and Fort Cumberland. d) The North Wall of Eastney Fort East with the barracks – Fort Cumberland track. Beyond are the playing fields and the housing built on the site of the old Hutment, later known as Melville and then Comacchio, Camp.

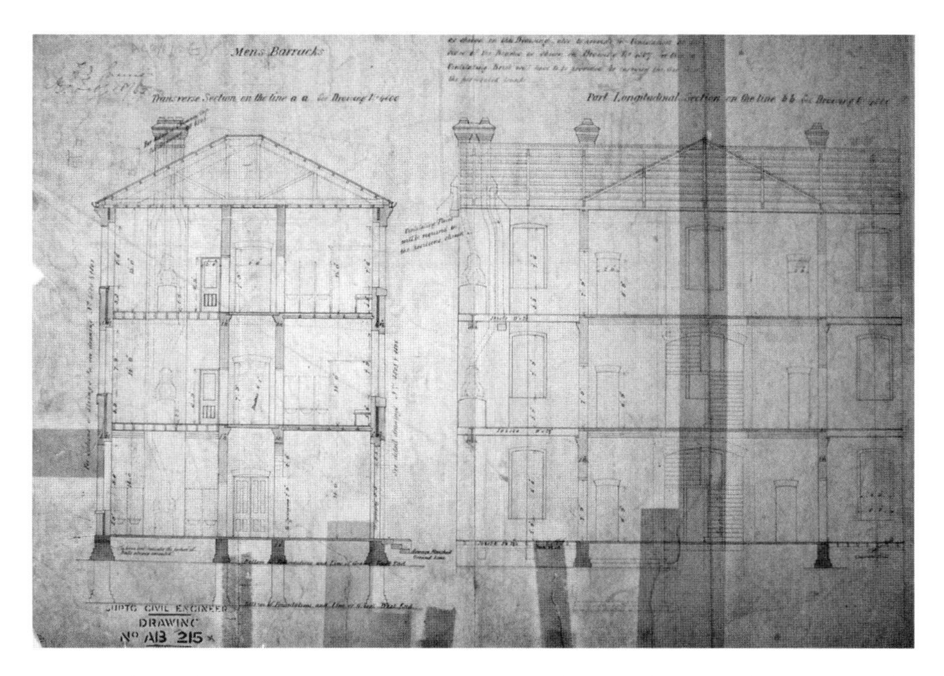

An example of the 1863 drawings of the men's barracks at Eastney.

sea beach, each containing two guns in cavalier bastions, and seven guns in embrasures. The whole is fronted and flanked by a deep ditch, having a low wall next to the scarp of the work for rifle fire. The scarp of the work itself is reverted with flints and concrete.'

The landward defences of the barracks were provided by a loop-holed wall which continued all round, apart from the front on the shoreline, where the forts and the connecting curtain closed the site.

The men's accommodation (now known as Gunners' Walk) was a long range facing the sea. It was made up of seven identical sections, each with a central stair with NCOs' rooms and washrooms off, flanked by cross-lit dormitories for twenty-four men. The roof was to be of Duchess Slate and there was a sophisticated venting system built into the flues and chimneys, which were to be finished with Jennings patented terracotta tops from Poole. The sergeants' messes, library, kitchens and separate dining rooms were in the basement. As with the Royal Marines Divisional barracks at Woolwich, this represented a much more progressive arrangement than was to be found in contemporary army barracks, especially in separating the eating and sleeping rooms of the men.

The layout of Eastney was a repeat of the previous new marines' barracks, at Chatham, Stonehouse and Woolwich, with the officers' accommodation being in detached wings at either side. The field officers' residence to the east was, like the marines' barracks of a century before, barely distin-

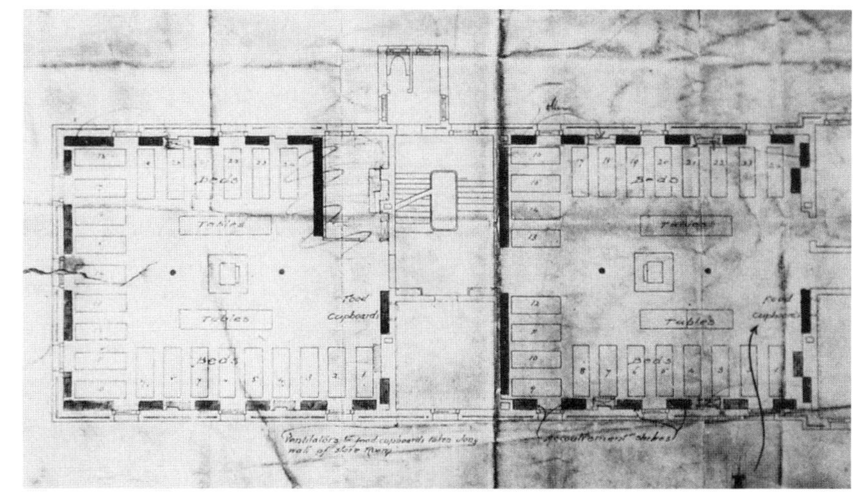

Plan showing the layout of the men's rooms of the main barrack block; note the provision for twenty-four beds.

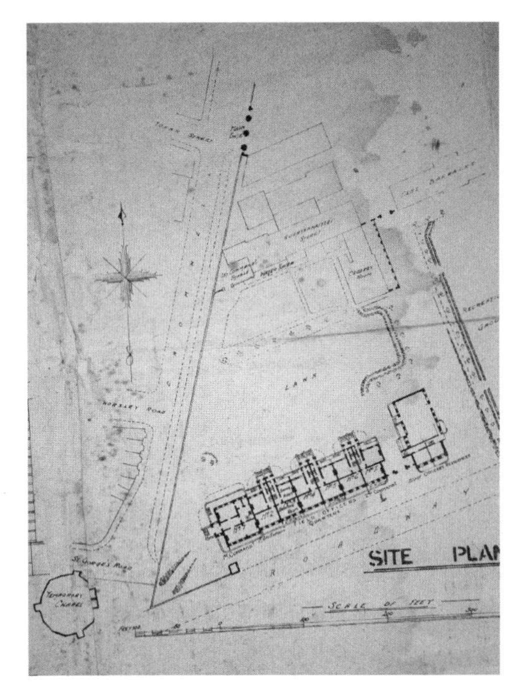

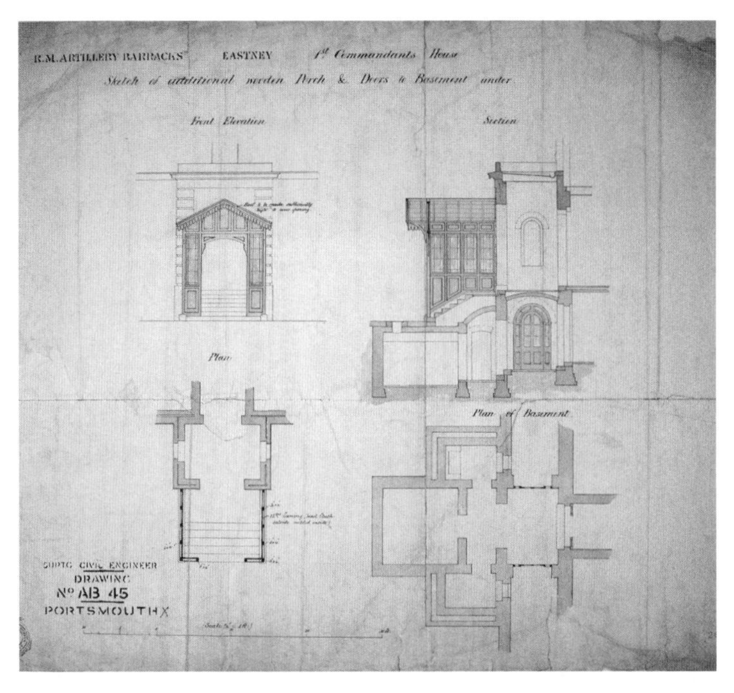

Left: Site plan showing the 1st and 2nd Commandants' residences flanking the Field Officers' quarters, with the Crinoline Church at the foot of St George's Road.

Right: The original drawings of the additional wooden porch built onto the Commandant's residence, dated 7th November 1868.

guishable from contemporary civilian terraces. The Officers' Mess at the opposite end of the parade ground was probably at this time the most imposing and architecturally refined in the kingdom. The central section was of Portland stone, with the entrance, on the piano nobile, approached by a grand, imperial stair. Italianate stone galleries were designed to ground and first floors with a balustrade parapet over the first floor gallery. Above the second floor was placed a balustrade parapet with an elaborately carved centre piece depicting the Royal Arms. The single officers' quarters either side were of three storeys, with a basement and attic, a mansard slate roof and dormers. They were constructed of red brick with yellow brick dressings.

The Commandant's horse and carriage outside Eastney House. The photograph is dated 1890, which if accurate, would indicate the occupants as being the family of Major-General John Crease RMA.

The main façade of the officer's mess, Eastney.

Beneath the stone steps to the Officers' Mess were two half door urinals for the use of officer's before attending parade.

Inside, the main dining room – the Mess Room – was the centre-piece of the whole building. The ceiling and mouldings feature gold leaf, and the fireplaces are of Italian marble. The Italian craftsmen left their mark by sculpting the Corps' motto incorrectly; it reads 'Per Mare Per Tere' (instead of 'Terram'). There are two fine crests between the balcony windows, one of the royal arms and the other of the Royal Marine Artillery. A parquet floor was fitted with inlaid corners. It is said that the accountant estimating the budget for this building placed one too many noughts, and that the error went undetected.

In the Hall, were the trophies and the medal collection, with the iron-work on the staircase incorporating globes of the corps crest, and the clear anchor, the badge of the Lord High Admiral. There are no Royal Navy

The dining room of the Officers' Mess at Eastney Barracks with one of the white Italian marble fire places at the south end.

Detail from the marble fireplace in the dining room of the Officers' Mess (now the RM Museum).

Detail of the wrought iron staircase in the Officers' Mess at Eastney. The Lord High Admiral's anchor of 1664 and the Globe of 1827 both feature, along with the Thistle of Scotland, Roses of England, and the Shamrock of Ireland. There is no heraldic device to represent Wales, as the country had been considered part of England since the reign of Edward I, and had no College of Arms or Welsh Heralds.

fouled-anchor emblems in any of the mess architecture. Upstairs in the mess were the card room, the library, and the billiard room in which there were two tables.

Continuing the trend of the new mess at Forton Barracks for Portsmouth Division RMLI, which had included an orchestra platform in an alcove on the main stairs, the Eastney Officers' Mess included a minstrels' gallery complete with glass opening doors on the mezzanine to act as a volume control. The central section was divided laterally by a full-height central stair hall extending the whole depth of the building, with a dignified staircase which rose in two flights to the minstrels' gallery. Eastney was the first of the seriously grandiloquent quarters which the British officer class built for itself during the second half of the nineteenth century, in which the Navy always outdid the Army.

Questions, however, were asked in the House of Commons about the wisdom of the design of the barracks in conjunction with the forts. In May 1864, while much of the barracks was still being built, Colonel Bartlett stood up in the Commons to state he thought the barracks were in a most 'untenable position' in the event of an attack from the sea. He thought it would have been safer for the men and their wives and families if the barracks had been built further inland, as the small forts might be bomb-proof but the three-storey barrack blocks would certainly not be.

Lord Paget, for the Government, replied that it was a good site for heavy guns and the men should reside near by and that the site had been obtained by the Admiralty, 'at very little expense'. The sea forts in the Solent, when finished, would offer protection.

Sir Frederick Smith said he thought he had never seen barracks worse situated – and they would cost £167,861 to build. Lord Paget confirmed that the estimate for building the barracks was £167,000, and added that if there was a war the men of the RMA would be at sea. The opposition protested that the men might be gone but their wives and children would be left undefended. A critic of the same date writes about them ' The new

The officers' dining room of the mess with the minstrels' gallery above the main arches.

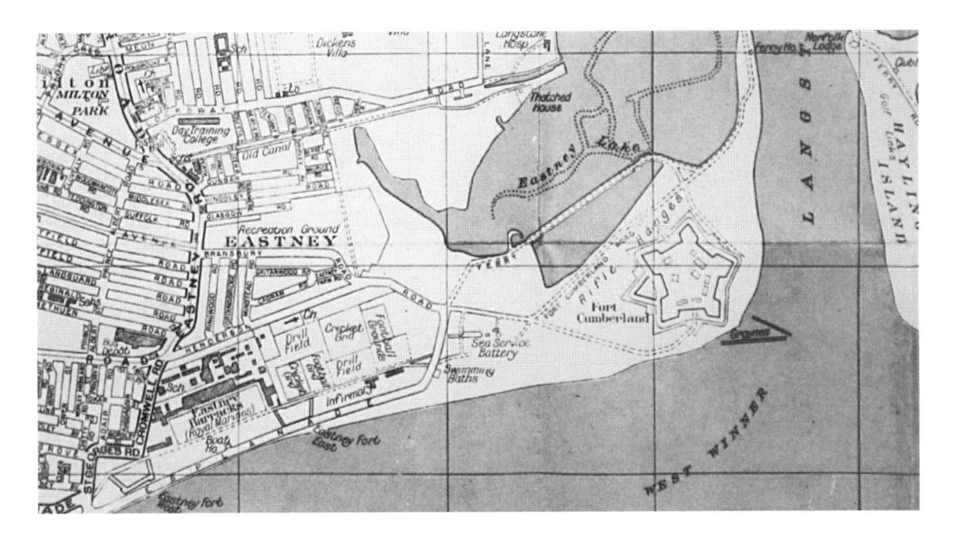

Section of a 1934 street map of Portsmouth showing the relative locations of Eastney Barracks, the sea service batteries and Fort Cumberland. Note that the southern section of the 'Glory Hole' at Eastney Lake, has yet to be filled in.

Barracks for the RMA at Portsmouth have just been commenced in the rear of a heavy Coast Fort commenced at the same time, and mounting guns of the largest calibre, so that in case of attack, all shots missing the batteries will plump right into the barracks.' The military counter to this observation was based on the experience that ships' gunners would tend to aim at what fired at them. Faced with two low profile batteries or a three storey block, it would be preferable to have fire decoyed away from the forts, to which the barracks was the more tempting target!

The 1869 report concerning the forts stated that the armament was five 7 inch breech loading guns and seven 8 inch smooth bore guns. The magazine accommodation was stated to be 'sufficient, but the provision for artillery stores is scarcely adequate'. The report continued.... 'as these batteries are at a great distance from the channel leading into Spithead and have a large extent of shoal water in front of them, they would take but little part in an engagement with large ships, and their present armament seems to be sufficient to keep small vessels or boats at a distance. For this purpose they have been skilfully constructed'.

As the forts neared completion, so the decision to place the barracks behind them was made, and in 1862 the land was prepared and materials gathered.

In December 1863 the contractor of Eastney Barracks complained of 'the great inconvenience caused by the numberless soldiers, in some cases accompanied by their wives and families, wishing to view the men's quarters'. These were the earliest buildings completed. In the recollections of Sergeant-Major J Hilson RMA, the first sergeant-major of the Royal Marine Artillery, he states 'in 1861 twenty-one acres of land were purchased to erect a barracks for the RMA. In 1864 the building of the barracks was slowly progressing, and by November the first block was ready for occupation. It was for the married people and was to accommodate ninety-two families, the ground floor being for colour-sergeants and 2nd class staff-sergeants (two rooms), other sergeants and rank and file on the first floor (one room). As several of the latter had some six, and in one case nine, children, one room

A section of stained glass from the Officers' Mess landing with the date of completion.

was not sufficient. The children above a certain age were sent to bed in the dormitories.'

On the 7th November, 1864, the first detachment marched in from Fort Elson, but it was not until the 1st April 1865, that any part of the new barracks was turned over to the Barrackmaster.

The colonnaded Orderly Room with married officers' quarters above.

Sergeant-Major Hilson continues '1865 – in the early part of this year, as the blocks in the main building were completed, they were occupied by the men being withdrawn from the fort (Fort Cumberland), A first, B second, and so on. There were no officers' quarters ready. The officers who were stationed at Eastney made themselves comfortable in what are now the Orderly and Court Martial rooms'.

The officers occupied G block for their mess and ante-rooms until the block comprising Officers' Mess and single officers' quarters was completed at the end of 1865. In 1894 the officers' mess was improved by the addition of a conservatory. Before this was built, the mess room was so cold that in the winter officers often had to wear their great coats at mess.

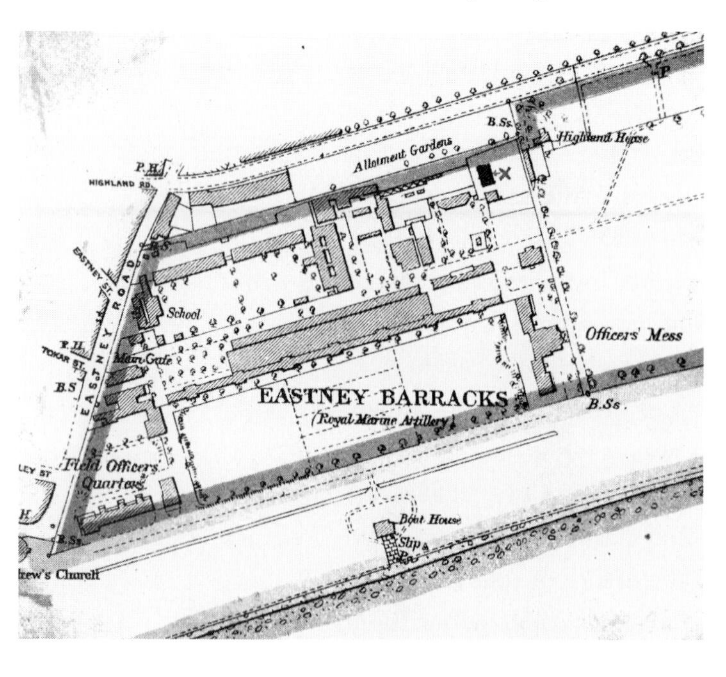

Site plan of Eastney Barracks in 1899.

A volunteer detachment from the Chatham and Woolwich Divisions, and the Band, soon followed, and the Canteen was set up in rooms 19 and 20 for the time being. There were quarters for four staff sergeants behind the guard-room, there being two, back to back, on either side of the armourer's shop, and in addition quarters for the paymaster's chief clerk above the pay office. The two quarters at the eastern end were occupied by the sergeants-major until 1899, when new houses were built for them in front of the provost sergeant's quarters; the old sergeants-major quarters became offices for the 1st and 3rd Quartermasters.

The field officers' quarters and the block of buildings containing the Commandant's office were built in 1866 and were nicknamed 'Teapot Row' and 'Scandal Alley' respectively: the former because of the regular sight of teapots being emptied, and the latter, for the gossip that accompanied the

The Provost Sergeant's house with the detention quarters to the left. Sergeant Edgar Bull RM lived here between 1944 and 1947 when this photograph was taken.

activity! Originally, besides the two married quarters on the south side there were two flats above the Commandant's office, the lower one being the Adjutant's quarters, and the top floor being usually allocated to a junior officer on the headquarter staff. By 1867 the RMA were in complete occupation of the barracks, including the married quarters and schools north of the

The RMA formed up on the parade at Eastney with oficers to the front. In the background can be seen the defensive parapet between Eastney Forts East and West, drainage ventilation shaft, and a sentry box at the entrance from the boathouse and slipway.

main block of buildings. The drill shed, detention quarters and officers' stables were also built.

The drainage was at first defective, and several deaths occurred from typhoid. Consequently a ventilation shaft was built between the parade ground and the sea, next to the boathouse. In 1868 a report by Surgeon

Rehearsal of the RMA at Southsea Common on 29th August 1880, for the inspection the following day by HRH Prince Edward of Saxe Weimar.

Robertson RN entitled "Health of the Navy" he remarked on the 'unwholesomeness and pestilential character of the dwellings in the neighbourhood of the barracks, which are almost wholly occupied by families belonging to Marine Artillerymen... In one street not a single house has a drain except into a piece of waste ground at the end of the row of houses. Some had a

Cesspool within a few yards of the back door.' It was perhaps typical both of the period, and of the lack of appreciation of the Corps in general, that there was no celebration or formal ceremony at the completion of this significant and striking building. Officers and men alike were simply moved in as accommodation for them became ready.

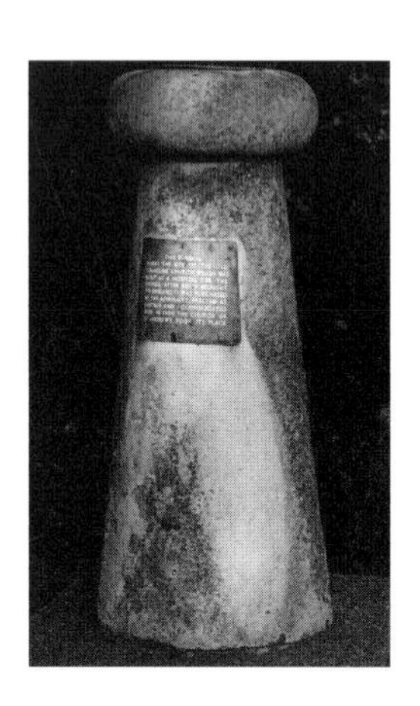

Originally a marker for the site of the Crinoline Church this stone sundial became a feature in the Commandant's garden in Eastney Fort West.

The Crinoline Church

The growth of Southsea in the 1850s had resulted in Thomas Ellis Owen designing and building St Jude's Church to serve the growing number of residents, but such was the pace of developments that further churches were going to be required. It was to fill this gap that a strange timber building was erected in 1858 on a circular plot of land in Outram Road. It was a twenty-sided building, 22 metres in diameter and 18 metres high, with its open-space interior lit by a great chandelier comprised of thirty-six lights – the design was originally intended as a field hospital for the Crimea War. The descending flare of the circular roof earned it the name of the 'Crinoline Church'. It wasn't only its shape that astonished local residents – the timber building was erected in only twenty-eight days, and served the community as St Bartholomew's for three years until the completion of a permanent stone-built church. The building was then purchased for £200, dismantled and re-erected in Waverley Road for a further £150, to serve as a temporary church while the brick-built St Simon's was completed. In 1864 it was reconstructed in St George's Road, Eastney, to the west of 'Teapot Row' and served as the barracks' church of St Andrew's, accommodating a congregation of 950, until the building of the new St Andrew's in Henderson Road in 1905. The bell was removed in 1906 to become the ship's bell for the Sea Service Battery, and the building was finally broken up in 1908, providing fire-wood until 1912.

The RMA Band leading the division from the Crinoline Church during church parade c1902.

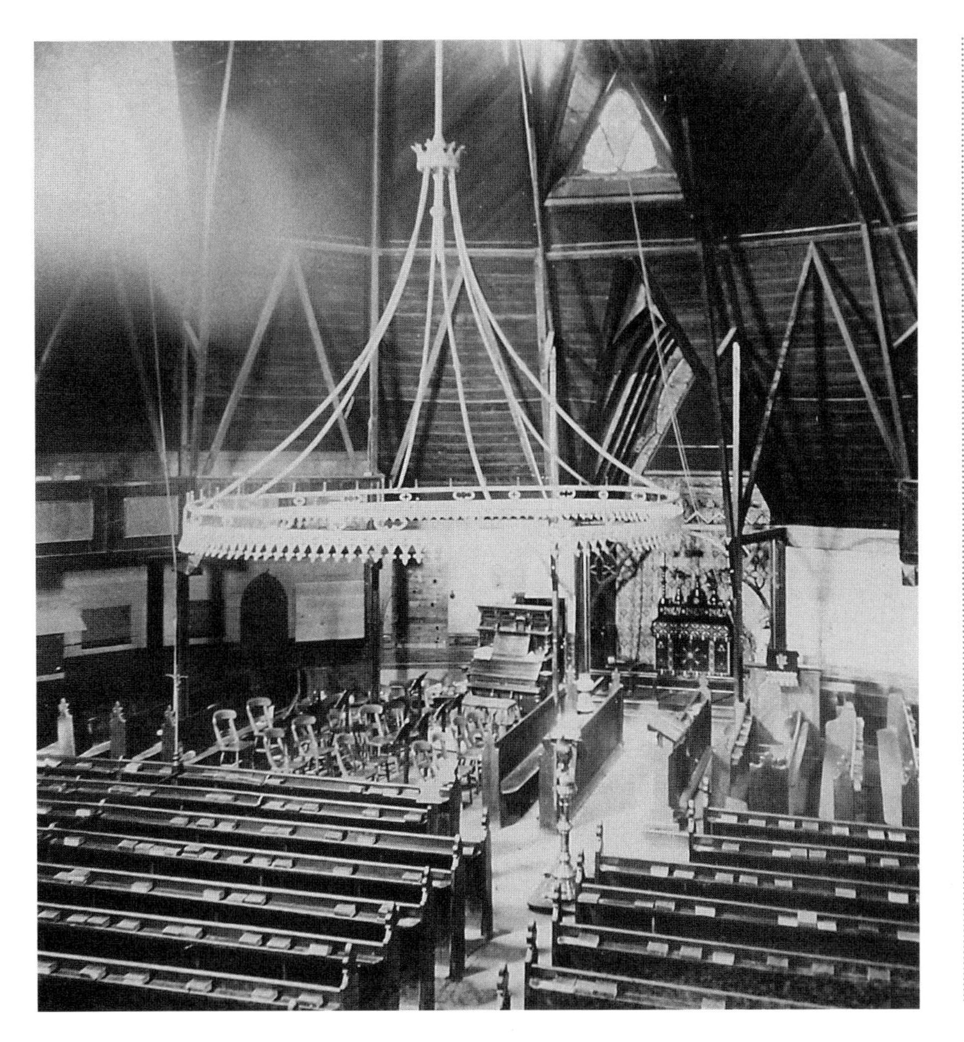

A rare interior view of the Crinoline Church with the altar and harmonium in the background.

Album photograph of the Crinoline Church with the Clock Tower in the background.

4 The Years of Expansion 1870 to 1913

THE FIRST commandant of Eastney Barracks was Colonel George Augustus Schomberg CB RMA, who was appointed 10 April 1867, and promoted to General in 1877. He and his successors oversaw the development of Eastney as a base for the Royal Marine Artillery and the training for its role for the next half a century. As well as the addition of buildings to the barracks itself, the land between the eastern wall, behind the Officers' Mess, to Fort Cumberland and the ferry point became training batteries and musketry ranges for sea service gunnery. In comparison the training within the fort itself was generally for land service artillery.

Ceremonial parade of the RMA, including the band, at Eastney Barracks for Queen Victoria's birthday 24th May 1869. This was probably the first parade of its type at this barracks.

The RMA had been using the drill battery on Southsea Common until 1859 when a battery was built at Eastney. It was placed near the cross cart roads to the northeast of the barracks, and contained 64 pdrs mounted on trucks. Practise was carried out from them at targets moored in the Langstone channel. This battery was known as the Garden Battery and the small pond to the south of it as the Garden Pond.

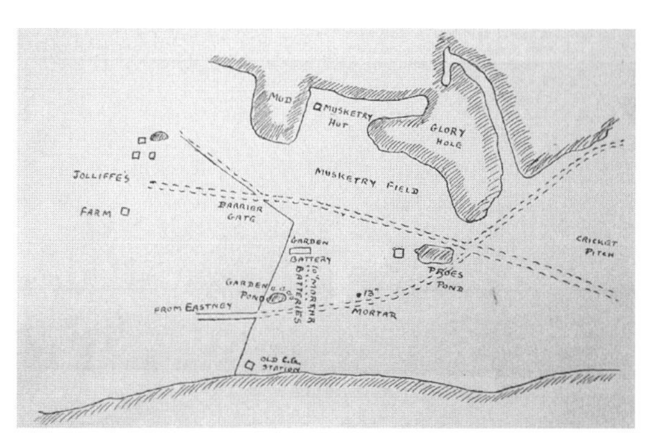

Pre 1896 sketch map showing Garden and Mortar Batteries in the area of Proe's Pond and Joliffe's Farm.

A contemporary report of the battery stated that, 'having "disarranged" the inspection of a Volunteer Battalion on an Easter Monday by lobbing solid shot in their direction, it met expostulation with the assurance that the RMA when at drill were treated in similar fashion, because it steadied the men under fire, and accustomed them to the dodging of shells'.

Near this battery, out in the open, were two 10 inch mortar batteries and one 13 inch mortar on a turntable, of the same pattern as those used in bomb-boats during the Crimean war. They were fired at a disc on a pole on the glacis near the south gate of Fort Cumberland, about 700 yards range. The mortar shells were only fired with a time fuse, and were collected for future use from where they happened to fall. The thirteen inch mortar was in later years placed at the sea entrance to Eastney parade ground, and is now in the RM Museum's collection.

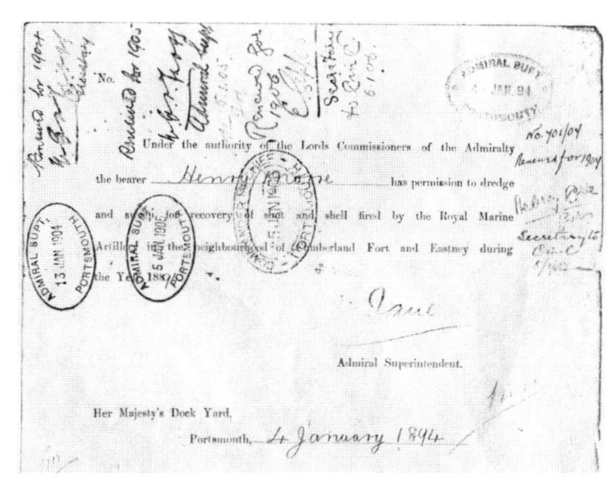
No.

Under the authority of the Lords Commissioners of the Admiralty the bearer Henry Moore has permission to dredge and sweep for recovery of shot and shell fired by the Royal Marine Artillery in the neighbourhood of Cumberland Fort and Eastney during the Year 189

Admiral Superintendent.

Her Majesty's Dock Yard,
Portsmouth, 4 January 1894

Licence for Henry Moore to dredge for shot fired from the practise batteries, over-stamped for consecutive years.

In 1871 drawings were produced for a new sea-service practise battery. The RMA had, for the last fifty or so years, been building various platforms in various locations, but this would be the most elaborate and substantial to date. It was designed with a curved deck floor and at a roofed height to resemble a gun-deck of an iron-clad ship of the time. It also had a semi-circular 'bow' at the eastern end. Inside were a variety of broad-side guns that would be encountered in the fleet such as one 10 inch, one 9 inch, one 8 inch RML, 64 pdr and some 7 inch guns. As the types of weapons changed

A collection of relics that were placed on the saluting dais side of the Parade ground c.1930. The brass cannon on the left was originally on the Parade at Forton Barracks until 1923, while the 13 inch 1855 mortar had been mounted on a practise turntable in 1859, at what is now Melville Road.

Sea Service Battery a) The original 1871 drawing (AB938) for the battery is held in the Museum Archive. b) An external photograph taken in 1914 from the south-east clearly shows its shape. c–e)During the early 1900s photographs were taken inside the battery. Although rather posed these provide valuable glimpses of the layout, the weapons and the drills. f-g)In 1908 photographs were taken that project a more earnest interpretation of the training. h) Another external view showing the Battery Instructional Staff of 1900.

or were improved, examples were installed and obsolete guns removed. By 1898 most of the muzzle loading guns had been replaced in the main battery by two 6 inch quick firing (QF) guns in casements, and one 4.7 inch QF.

In 1886 a smaller wooden structure, similar to the bow end of this building, was replicated inside Eastney Barracks, north east of the gymnasium and mounted 6 inch breech loading guns, although the drawings indicated piercings for three 9 ton 8 inch weapons. Titled the 'New Gun Drill Battery', it was at first used for recruit classes prior to them using the sea service battery. This had come about due to the RMA being able to recruit directly, as opposed to transferring suitable Royal Marine recruits from the divisions. RMA recruits would be ranked as 'Private' until passing a sixty-eight day gunnery course to qualify them as 'Gunner'. The building was later used for spotting and deflection teaching, and prior to the First World War, the guns were removed and the building was used as the Brigade Depot Quartermaster's store and office. In January 1921 it became the shoemakers' shop before being demolished.

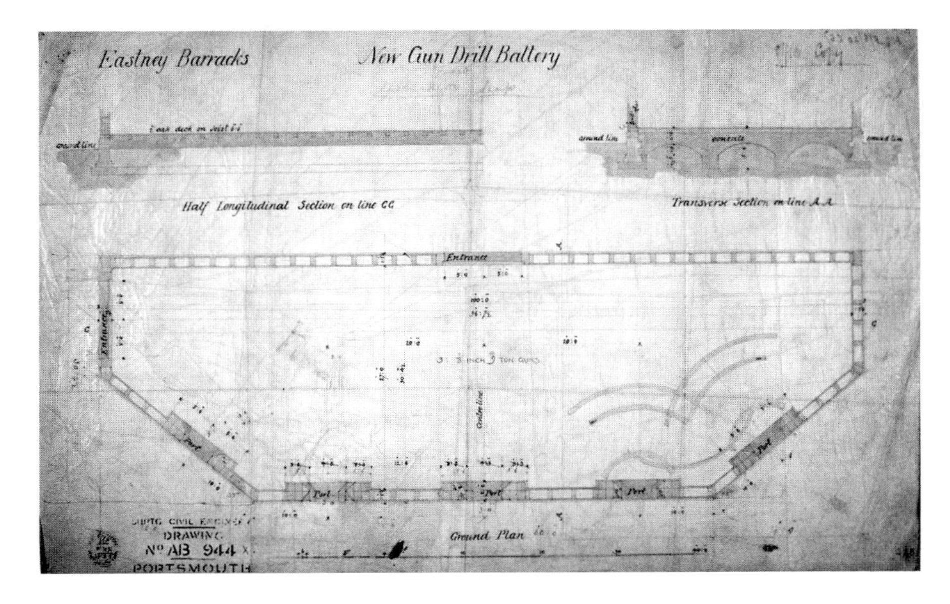

Below Left: The original drawing of the practise battery built within the barracks in 1886.

Bottom Left: Buildings to the North of the main Barrack Block include the 1886 Sea Service Battery which then became the Shoemakers Shop until 1939. This building has angular corners and is located right of centre towards the bottom. Below this and to the right is the Detention Block. Left of this is the Provost Sergeants Building and then the Warrant Officers Quarters. Halfway up the page and running across it is the Men's Institute. Above that are two similar Dining Halls and, in between, the cookhouse. At the top of the picture, with two towers, is the stores building that, in Victorian times, was the Eastney Barracks School. Part of this building became the first Royal Marines Museum.

Bottom right: The 9.2 inch breech loading centre pivot Vavasseur gun on its special mounting (see adjacent drawing No AB920) with two mobile machine guns in front. Photograph taken before the building was fully clad suggesting that it was taken at about the time of the guns installation in 1893. The building to the left is probably the housing for the 3 pdr Hotchkiss.

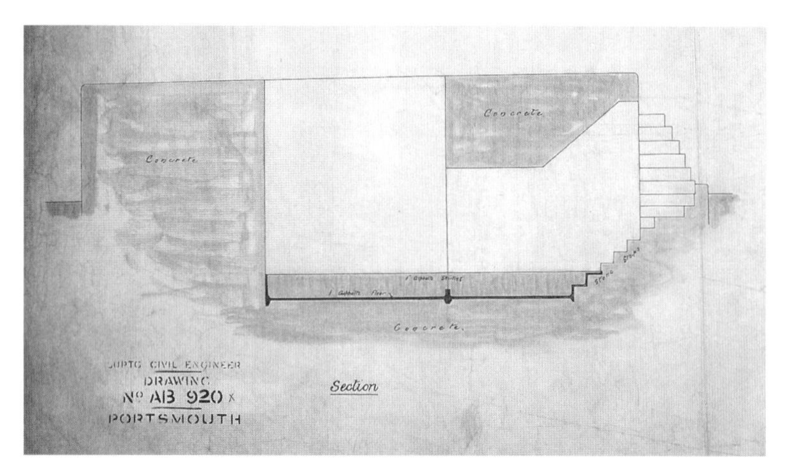

The chamber emplacement plan for the 9.2 inch centre-pivot Vavasseur gun, placed to the east of the sea service battery. Named after its inventor, engineer Joseph Vavasseur (1834–1908), these guns were amongst the first to use hydraulics to control recoil and return the gun to its position after firing.

In 1893 a Vavasseur 9.2 inch centre-pivot BL gun was mounted in a firing position (en barbette) east of the main battery near Proe's Pond. This gun was one of the largest calibre hand operated types when mounted and was used by the RMA for drill. It was also included in the overall area defence scheme, although never actually fired live.

In 1896 an ammunition room, with offices for the instructor staff was built between the main and garden batteries, and a machine gun battery between the main battery and the 9.2 inch. In it was a 3 pdr Hotchkiss mounted on a revolving platform. Firing was carried out to sea, and the noise from the corrugated-iron roof and sides was deafening.

The Garden Battery was demolished when these new buildings were taken over, and as soon as the demolition was complete the old mortar parapet was levelled and the Garden Pond filled in.

The period between 1902 and 1913 was one of significant modernisation and reform in the Royal Navy in both ship technology and manning. The introduction of power operated gunnery with central fire control, and wireless telegraphy into the new *Dreadnought* class fleet, required the Royal Marines to provide skilled detachments for naval gunnery. These new ships needed larger crews and in 1901 the Royal Fleet Reserve had been formed, as a method of recalling trained seamen and marines upon mobilisation.

Perhaps the most spectacular addition to the sea-service batteries was a huge two storey 'ships' gun turret constructed in 1912. It mounted two different types of 12 inch gun; the right gun was of the Mark IX type used in the HMS *Irresistible* class of battleship, while the left gun was a version of the Mark IX used in the HMS *King Edward VII* class warships. To add realism, the turret traversed and would 'pitch and roll'

Although rather indistinct the background of this image shows the officers' mess on the skyline. In front of it is the wooden Sea Service Battery. To the left of this is the small building that housed the 3pdr Hotchkiss and, further left, the larger building which could be the location of the 9.2inch B.L. gun. Behind this can be seen the tall infirmary. To the right of the SSB can be seen the small Armourer's Shop and the larger Marsden Shed.

The new 12 inch gun turret provides a suitable, and dramatic, backdrop to the members of a c.1912 sea service gunnery course.

The 12 inch turret required large amounts of steam to power it so a separate boiler and engine house was built at the same time. This rare image shows the steam engine and the staff required to operate and maintain it.

to simulate the movement of a ship; the whole structure was powered by a steam engine salvaged from the old battleship HMS *Colossus* (1886-1908). The turret would have two gun-layers teaching eight men per gun and shells would be brought up on proper hoists, rammed into the barrel, and the breech closed. After 'firing,' the shell was manually pushed along the barrel until it dropped through a special aperture into the distinctive retrieval shute and was fed back to the magazine ready for the next practice. The breeches

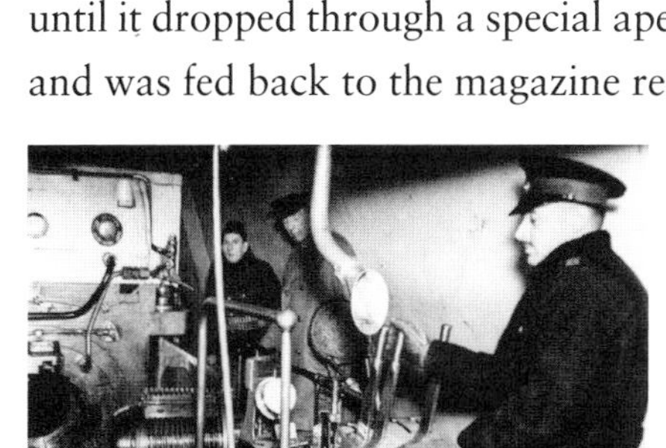

Left: Mr Castles, the turret engineer, watches as an RMA Instructor operates the right-hand 12 inch gun in the turret.

Right: Two turrets were built at HMS *Excellent* on Whale Island in 1902 for the instruction of Royal Navy Gunnery officers and men. They did not have the chute system of shell recovery. The power house can be seen between the turrets.

of the guns were later modified to simulate 15 inch guns, and for many Royal Marines over the next forty or so years, it became known as 'the home of the screaming skulls'.

The RMA were also expected to complete musketry courses, so ranges were constructed in this area of Eastney in addition to the sea-service gunnery. In 1885 a 600 yard range was in use, with four iron plate targets, and from drawings provided in 1884, a light railway was constructed with chain linked moving targets that were hand winched from a protected safe distance. In 1887 Blands Butts designed and named after Lieutenant James Fox Bland (1827-1893) of the 76th Regiment, and No. 4 Musketry Hut were completed. With the issue of the .303 inch rifle in 1895 it was found that the existing range was no longer safe, and in 1896-7 the dockyard constructed an eight canvas target range, with a huge stop butt behind, and at the same time built a "floating" road on faggots across the mud, to divert the Hayling Island traffic during such times as firing was taking place. This range was lengthened to 800 yards, the last 200 yards being reclaimed from the 'Glory Hole'. Prior to this, the old Mortar Butt on the glacis near the south gate of Fort Cumberland was used when firing at 800 yards. In 1902 a 1,000 yards firing point was built to give practise to skilled shots, and a small four-target range of two mantlets, fitted with four Spencer targets, was constructed to the eastward of the main range and running back to 500 yards. The targets and other features of the ranges were heavily influenced by Earl Spencer, who was a founder member of the National Rifle Association, and what later became the Hythe School of Musketry. This range enabled recruits and trained soldiers to carry out practices at the same time, and also offered greater facilities for naval and military units to carry out musketry courses on the Eastney range. Between 1912-3, the main range was extended by the addition of eight more targets on the east end of the existing butt.

Painting of Proe's Cottage in 1863 by Lieutenant Cuthbert Suther RMA, showing Fort Cumberland in the background. This building was adjacent to the farm and on the death of Mrs Proe became the quarters of the Instructor of Musketry, Staff Sergeant Rowlatt RMA. Suther went on to become Commandant of the RMA at Eastney in May 1891.

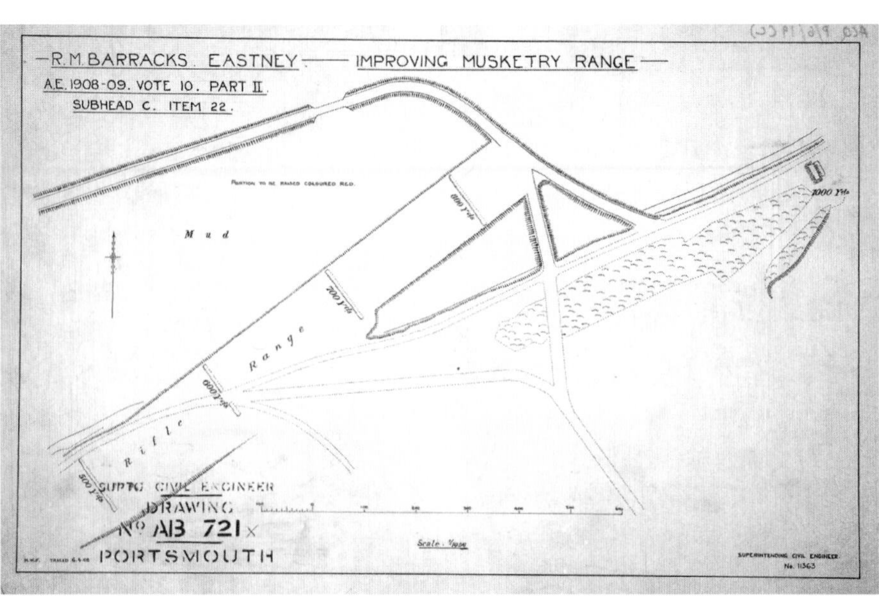

1909 drawing showing the improvements to the musketry ranges and also the 'alternative' road for public access to the Hayling Island ferry whilst firing was taking place.

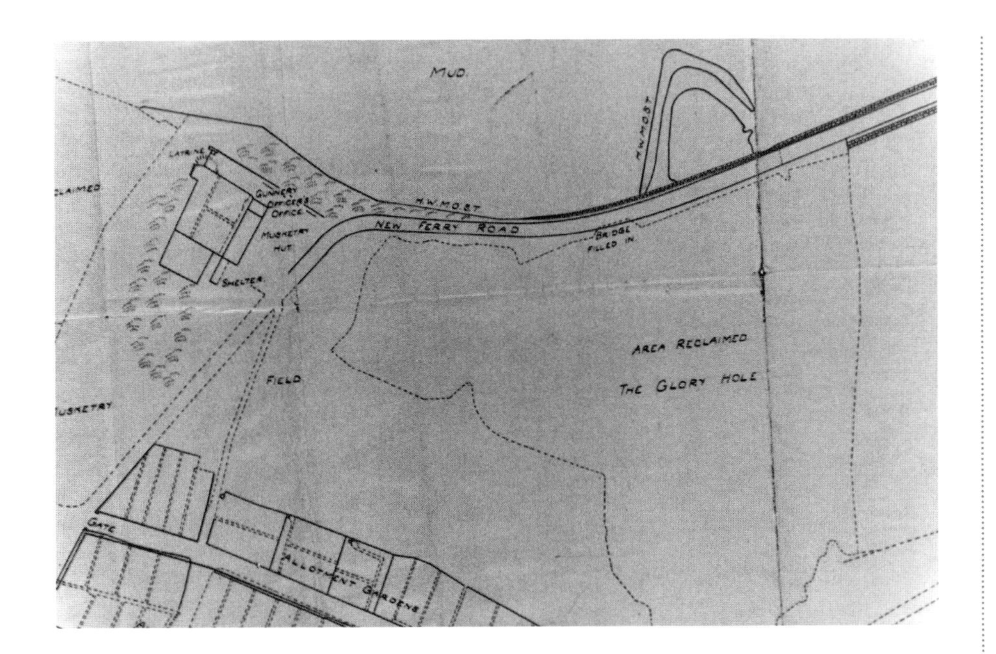

Map showing the Musketry Hut and related buildings plus the extent of land reclaimed from 'The Glory Hole'.

Taken in 1900 this picture of repository drill on the Right Bastion shows interesting detail in the background. On the left horizon can be seen the fort's ravelin. In the centre are the targets on one of the musketry ranges whilst, far right, can be seen the outline of the Eastney Barracks Officers' Mess.

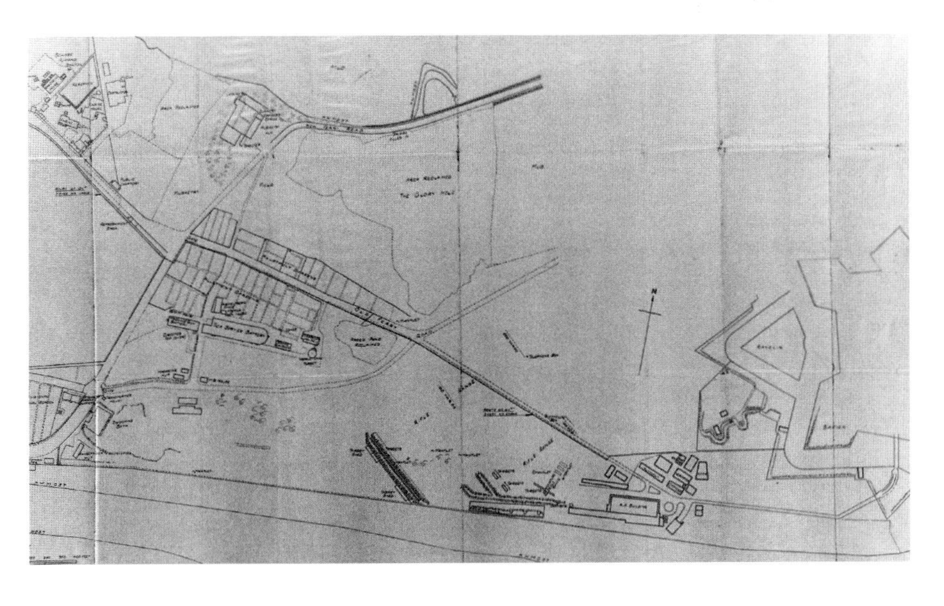

This 1944 map provides a useful guide to the relative locations of Fort Cumberland, the Sea Service Battery and Gunnery School and the ranges, as well as the swimming pool, the sewerage pumping station and Fraser Battery – here shown as 'AA Building'. Note also the large numbers of allotments.

A view across to the Eastney Sewerage Pumping Station with the large chimney of the refuse destructor. In front of this is the Musketry Hut and the Gunnery Officer's office. Low tide clearly shows the deep water channels of Eastney Lake. To the right, behind the shear-legs can be seen the buildings of Locksway Road including the St James' Hospital complex. Three white strips between the parapet wall and the water are musketry range firing positions, probably (from left to right) the 200, 300 and 400yd positions. The bridge for the roadway that bypasses the ranges can be clearly seen.

Back at Eastney, it was in 1870 that the most prominent landmark of the barracks was constructed, set south of the main gate behind the guard room and armoury. The water tower was built six storeys high to provide sufficient head of water pressure for fire fighting purposes, and square in plan, with a stair tower to the east. Built of brick in an Italianate style and battered out at the base, it was designed with white stone sills and string courses and a white stone corbel table supporting the upper storey.

In 1872 it was decided to place a clock mechanism, with faces on each side, in the storey containing the water tank. The clock from Woolwich Dockyard was found to be suitable and had been acquired by John Moore & Sons for renovation. The clock was an 'Eight day quarter Turret clock' originally built by William Dutton in 1784 and was similar to one placed in the Deptford yard. Four eight foot dials; two skeletons, and two of convex copper were installed with leads through the tank at low level. The chimes were organised with ting-tang on the quarters and full chime on the hour – all on one bell. A fourteen foot, two second pendulum, and a one and a half hundred- weight cast iron lenticular bob, were the other mechanical features of this movement. Not long after the installation, it was regarded as one of the best time keepers in the city.

All of this nearly came to grief when, on the 21st December 1922, a fire broke out on the ground floor of the clock tower that damaged the floor of the master tailor's store on the first floor. A corner stove was over fed and the resulting flue fire ignited the floor that the stack passed through. Fortunately the fire was contained before ascending further upwards.

A very large muzzle loading gun barrel appears to teeter on the bastion edge as two teams of men work hard on the capstans to drag it along the wall. In the background can be seen the Eastney Pumping Station and the musketry buildings with the water of 'The Glory Hole' between them and the fort. The posts running from the spit of land to the right edge of the picture would appear to be the markers for the roadway built to allow the extension to the musketry ranges – an early by-pass. One of the musketry range firing positions can be seen to the left of the figure in the dark uniform.

Early Flight at Eastney a) The first aircraft to land in Portsmouth was piloted by Lt G V Wildman-Lushington RM.When the Central Flying School opened at Upavon in 1912 he was one of three Royal Marine Officers on the course, all of whom were awarded their flying certificates in December 1912. Posted to the Naval Wing of the Royal Flying Corps at Eastchurch he gave dual instruction to Winston Churchill, the First Lord of the Admiralty. Posted to HMS *Hermes* he was based at the Isle of Grain. b) He visited Eastney on a number of occasions and would take-off across the musketry range between the 100 and 200 yard firing points and the Fort Glacis. c) A temporary hanger was built for him on the seaward side of the Sea Service Battery and in this picture the 12 inch Instructional Turret and the power house can be seen in the background. d) He died in a flying accident in December 1913 and was buried, with full military honours, in Christchurch Cemetery on Portsdown Hill.

The water tower shortly after completion in 1870, prior to the clock being installed. Seated wearing a top hat is the first Commandant at Eastney, Colonel George Schomberg RMA, with his family.

View of the married (later staff) officers' quarters with the Crinoline Church to the left and clock tower to the right of the picture.

View of Eastney Barracks from the south-west c1890. The Crinoline Church, clock tower, and Teapot Row can be seen with Eastney Fort West in the foreground. Note the esplanade road has yet to be built.

The lawns and shrubberies around the barracks were laid out under the direction of General Barnard, CB, when Commandant between 1870 and 1872. In 1865 RMA fatigue parties had constructed the road from the Barrier Gate to Eastney Barracks, the hedge being planted and gardens laid out at the same time. The Parade Ground was completed four years later. The men's (gunners) lawn, which had at various periods been used as a drill ground, and football and hockey pitches, was re-conditioned in 1921 and laid out as tennis courts.

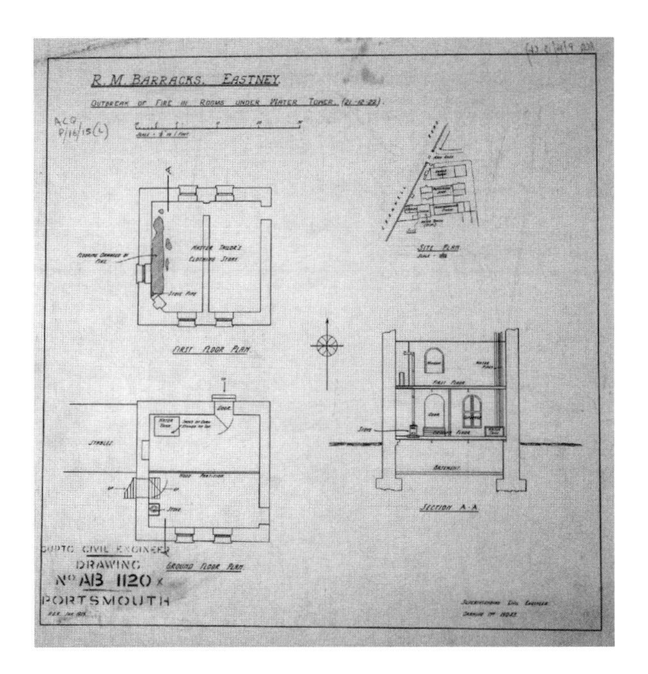

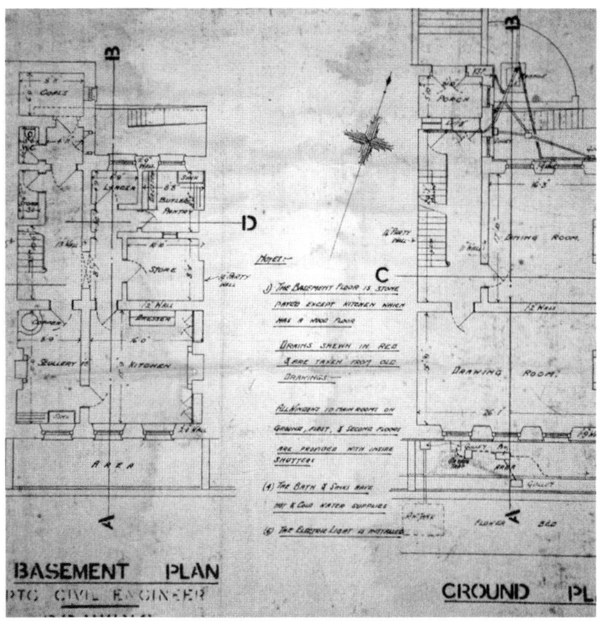

Left: Plan of the damage to the master tailor's store in the clock tower caused by the fire in December 1922.

Right: Detail from the field officers' residences with room layouts. These drawings were produced in 1905-6 when electric lighting was being introduced to the buildings. Rain water tanks are also shown in front of alternating basements, which were the work place for the servants.

Further building additions to the barracks were as follows:

- 1886 Carpenters' shop and shooting gallery.
- Blacksmiths' shop.
- Gymnasium.
- 1892 Band practice room and tailors' shop.
- 1893 Clothing shed between the store and armourers' shop.
- 1900 New boiler house.
- 1901 The old married quarters were converted to single men's quarters. The recruits, then four hundred and fifty in number, were transferred to these buildings, where the recruits occupied the major portion whilst HQ companies were in the remainder.
- 1905 A Telephone Exchange was installed in the barracks and situated in the guard-room. The swimming baths and Technical Training Instruction Room were built, along with the new Pay Office building.

The Main Parade Ground at Eastney in 1884. The grass in the foreground has yet to become established. At this period the RMA were deployed to the campaigns in Egypt and the Soudan.

The lawns and tennis courts in front of the Officers' Mess, 1902. Bowls and croquet were played to the left of this picture. Towards the western end of the parade ground the 'men's' lawn was marked out as a football pitch in some early photographs.

Internal view of the gymnasium at Eastney, built in 1898. Fencing foils and masks adorn the walls, whilst the lighting is provided with umbrella gas fittings. The photograph is from an album dated 1902-04.

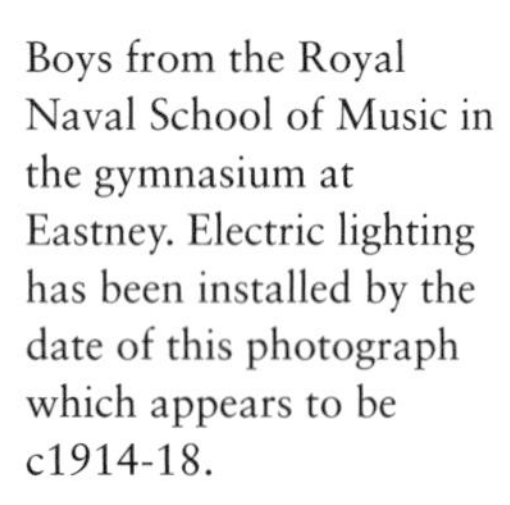

Boys from the Royal Naval School of Music in the gymnasium at Eastney. Electric lighting has been installed by the date of this photograph which appears to be c1914-18.

A group of RMA post and delivery NCOs c.1890.

On July 22nd, 1903, the Royal Naval School of Music was formed at Eastney and took over part of the eastern half of the old married quarters (K block). The first party consisted of thirty-four ratings from HMS *Impregnable* and HMS *Lion*, under Bandmaster Lidiard. By 1908 the RN Bands had been concentrated at Eastney and took over H block in addition, and in the course of time the whole of the buildings.

Prior to 1866 part of an old building in Fort Cumberland was used as a hospital, but after that year an infirmary was built in Eastney Fort East. In 1881 the new infirmary was built to a design by Major-General Percy Lewellin Smith RE (1838-1893) and included a two storey annex complete with a central hot water system designed by Rosser & Russell of Charing Cross.

One that got away. Gunners apprehensively watch the flight of a heavy gun barrel as it topples from its position balanced on top of a gun-carriage. The original Fort Cumberland hospital is in the background.

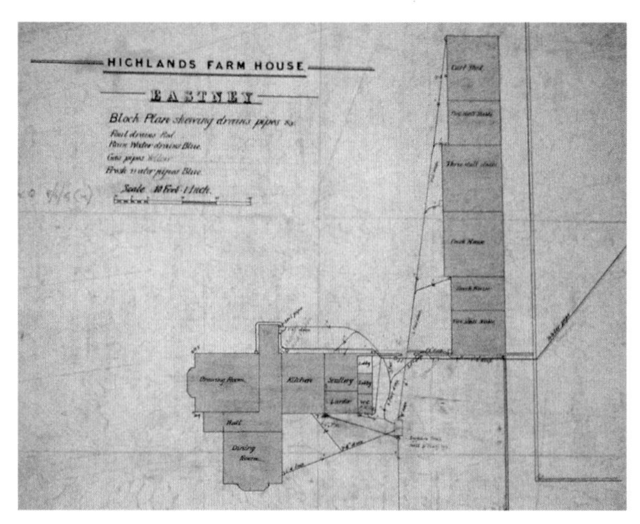

Left: View of the infirmary built at Eastney in 1881. Further along the road which is built on top of the original track to Fort Cumberland, are the staff sergeants' quarters and the old gunnery laboratory.

Right: Plan of Highland House with adjacent stables. Many drivers in Portsmouth will have passed nervously through its' doors as it became the driving test centre after the barracks closed.

In 1900 a disinfector was installed, and in 1918, after the influenza epidemic, a spraying chamber was built. In 1904 the dispensary and women's waiting rooms were completed. Formerly a portion of the building between the schools and the old married quarters was used for this purpose, with an entrance from between the main gate and the coal shed, opposite the guard room.

Highland House, in Henderson Road, was bought by the Crown and converted into a Quartermaster's residence in 1888, and remained so until 1892. It then became the 'sick house' for married families between 1892 and 1904, after which date a house in Highland Road was used. The foreman of works took the empty house over in 1907 and in 1926 it became the Chaplain's house due to the proximity of St Andrew's Church.

Lithograph of the drawing and plan of the new St Andrew's Church for Eastney Barracks, dated February 1904.

In 1905 the Church of St Andrew was completed and took the place of the old 'Crinoline' structure, which stood on the ground between the field officers' quarters and the officers' gardens. The foundation stone of the new church was laid by HRH the Princess of Wales on the 16th March, 1904, and was dedicated by the Lord Bishop of Winchester on the 17th November, 1905. It was constructed of Rowlands Castle red bricks, with

Top left: The laying of the foundation stone of the new St Andrew's Church by HRH The Princess of Wales in 1904.

Top right: HRH The Prince of Wales inspects the RMA on the Main Parade.

Left: Departure of HRH The Prince and Princess of Wales from Eastney in 1904. The stone bollard in the foreground was moved with one on the opposite side of the stairs, to Fort Cumberland and placed at the sea gate.

Portland and Bath stone dressing. It could accommodate one thousand people, and was of the early English style of architecture with similarities to other naval churches built around this time. They were generally known as 'Admiralty Pattern Churches'. As far as is known the church was never consecrated. The reredos was erected with money from the RMA War Memorial Fund.

The stone bollard now at the sea gate of Fort Cumberland.

The Signal School at this time was situated in a building called Ivy Cottage which had originally been built as a mess for naval ranks from HMS *Excellent* when undertaking field gun training on the Eastney ranges.

In 1889, Portsmouth Corporation wanted ground east of Fort Cumberland for an outfall and tanks for their drainage system. By

Stained Glass designs for the new St Andrew's Church at Eastney, dated 9th July 1912.

RMA Church Parade 1904, with Band and Buglers to the left.

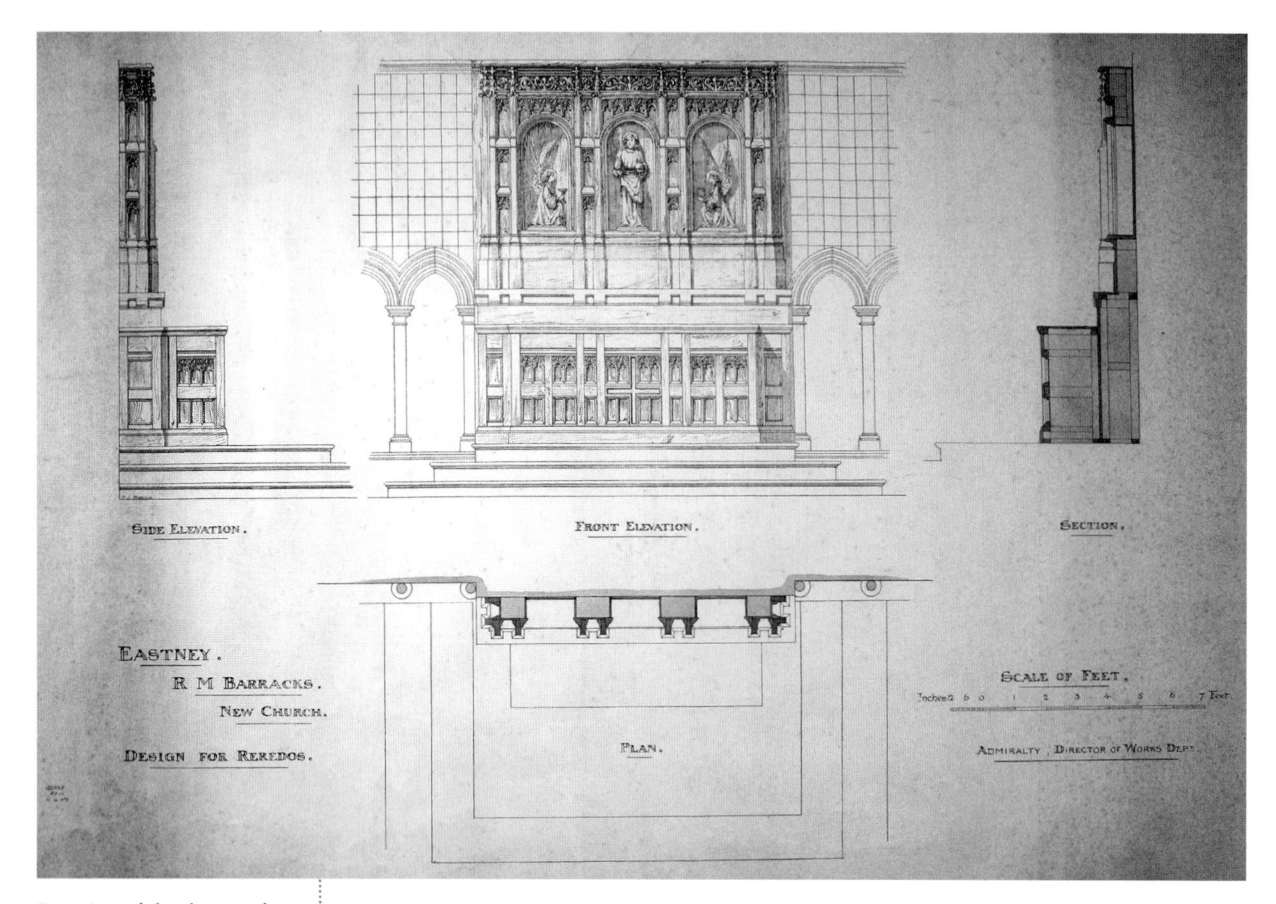

Drawing of the design of the reredos of St Andrew's Church, Eastney.

Baptism certificate of Evelyn Mary Brown, baptised in St Andrew's Church on Easter Day 1909.

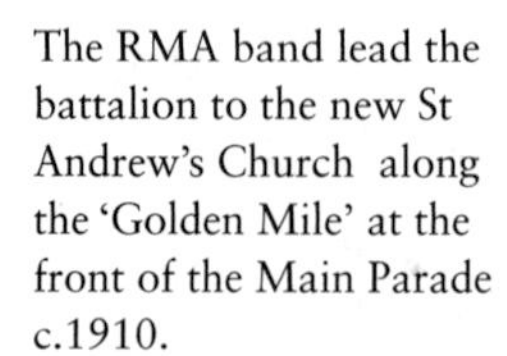

The RMA band lead the battalion to the new St Andrew's Church along the 'Golden Mile' at the front of the Main Parade c.1910.

A casual photograph taken after Sunday Church Parade at Eastney c1890. The RMA band play standing in a circle on the parade.

way of an exchange with the government, they purchased an arable field of thirty-three acres from Jolliffes' Farm whose land extended to the north beyond the present Henderson Road, and this became the barracks drill field. Towards the eastern end of the barracks an earthwork was constructed on this drill field, partly for instruction and partly as a defensive work which was used to practise 'the attack'. Known as 'Suther's redoubt', it was not remarkably successful and was levelled in 1898, however a platform was built outside the Officers' Mess

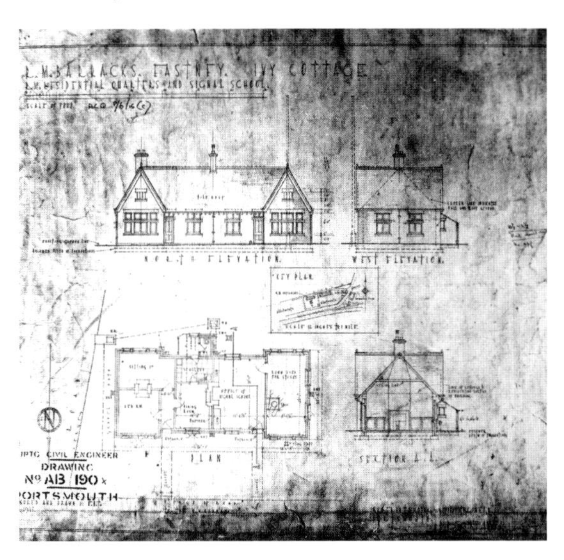

Ivy Cottage, built as a Signal School and residential quarters in 1933.

View looking east on the barrack road, with the cinema, squash court, gymnasium entrance, with the Wrens' block in the background.

dining room windows as an observation area for overlooking the exercises carried out. The platform was later used as the base for the conservatory added there in 1894, and the drill field later became the playing fields.

One of the most notable users of this platform was Kaiser Wilhelm II on his visit to Eastney on August 7th 1890. As part of his stay with Queen Victoria at Osborne House, he boarded the Royal Yacht *Alberta* at Cowes and landed at Eastney, where 'After various presentations, the Emperor and

View of the sports field and the rear of the Officers' Mess at Eastney, including the glass conservatory. The crane to the right is beginning the building of the Wrens accommodation block.

party crossed the dry moat to the parade ground of the Royal Marine Barracks, with a guard from the Yorkshire Regiment, while the band played the National Anthem, followed by 'The Watch on the Rhine'. At the steps leading to the officers' mess was a guard of honour consisting of one hundred men of the Royal Marine Artillery, under command of Captain Pease. Here a luncheon was prepared by Colonel Crease and the officers of the division; the chair was occupied by the Duke of Edinburgh as head of the Royal Marines.'

The Duke of Edinburgh, who was first awarded the title 'The Captain-General' of the Royal Marines; the title was passed to the next Duke, HRH Prince Phillip.

After this meal the Kaiser witnessed a mock attack conducted by the RMA, the Inniskilling Fusiliers, and 46th Mounted Battery, with two companies of RMLI and a Nordenfeldt machine gun providing the defence. The purpose was to demonstrate Colonel Crease's tactical invention of smoke bombs and shells to obscure the attack from defenders with protective cover and machine guns. This was a prophetic display of what was to be attempted some twenty-four years later, with catastrophic results. The Kaiser remarked 'the British Royal Marine is the best all round fighting man in the world' before departing back to Cowes. He made one further visit to Eastney before the First World War; it was on the 11th November, 1907.

Kaiser Wilhelm II inspecting the RMA Guard of Honour and Band by the South Railway Jetty, Portsmouth Harbour in 1907. He later visited and dined at Eastney.

5 The RMA Division at Eastney

THE INTERNAL organisation of the RMA Division at Eastney is perhaps worthy of examination, and a good account was produced by the last Adjutant of the RMA, Colonel George W M Grover OBE RM. It was produced on the occasion of a re-union of former RMA Officers and men at Eastney in 1965, and the section describing the division is quoted in its entirety.

'The RMA, Eastney, differed in some details from its Light Infantry counterparts, and this description is as it stood in 1923 when the amalgamation of the corps took place. At the head was the Commandant, Brigadier-General or Colonel Commandant as he became after the First World War. Next was the Colonel Second Commandant, Examiner of accounts, a down-trodden functionary forever flitting from place to place in quest of irregularities which might range from a disgruntled gunner flinging himself from the clock tower without damage to anything more important than the forage en route for the stables, to a missing tuppence in the clothing accounts. There were two staff officers, originally styled the Office and Field Adjutants, although for many years the former, a Major, had been styled Brigade Major. His office was a large one with a superintending clerk and a variety of lesser functionaries as, apart from conducting the current affairs of the Division, his department held all records of past and serving ranks of the RMA Division. The second of these two, the Adjutant—the expression "Field" having been dropped, similarly had other duties than those of a normal unit Adjutant in that he kept the rosters and quarterly reports of all NCOs and candidates for promotion both ashore and afloat who, up to the rank of Staff Sergeant, were promoted by the Commandant as vacancies arose. His "company" which was, in lean times, stronger than any of the parade companies, occupied an entire barrack block and comprised the bands of Headquarters and the Royal Yacht, the corps of drums and the regimental police. Under him were the parade and office Sergeants Major, the QMSI instructor of infantry and the infantry parade staff. Further, since the RMA trained its own recruits, there was an Adjutant, Recruits Depot. On the instructional side were the instructors of gunnery—Sea Service, Land Service, Coast Defence and Repository—and the instructor of musketry. On the administrative side were three Quartermasters, the First, clothing, the Second, ordnance, and the Third, rations and transport. Retired officers filled the posts of Barrack-master and Paymaster. An infirmary dealt with the sick and those of families, staffed by three RN surgeons and their acolytes, specially trained NCOs and gunners. Since, in the old days, motor cars were a rarity and officers with their wives lived locally, as did the married other ranks, the district formed a closely knit community and the task, now given the somewhat pretentious name of "welfare", of sorting out the troubles entailed by separation of families, largely solved itself.'

One of the examples of the 'welfare' referred to by Colonel Grover dated from the 1870s. "Major Little's Fund" was initiated after the £6 annual interest on a legacy bequeathed by the late Major Simon Ridley Little RM was received from the charity commission. On 1st November 1876, notice was given by the Colonel Commandant, George Digby RMA, that a fund be set up at Eastney. Officers would contribute unsolicited subscriptions or donations for post office investment to allow charitable awards for the temporary relief of widows and children of NCOs and men dying while in service or deserving families that had sickness to contend with. Names of those thought to be in distress would be passed to the Chaplain by company officers from time to time who would then recommend those fitting to the Colonel Commandant. A similar fund called 'The Chatham Chest' had existed at that division in the early nineteenth century where officers donated a days pay to the 'chest' for the benefit of families of men killed.

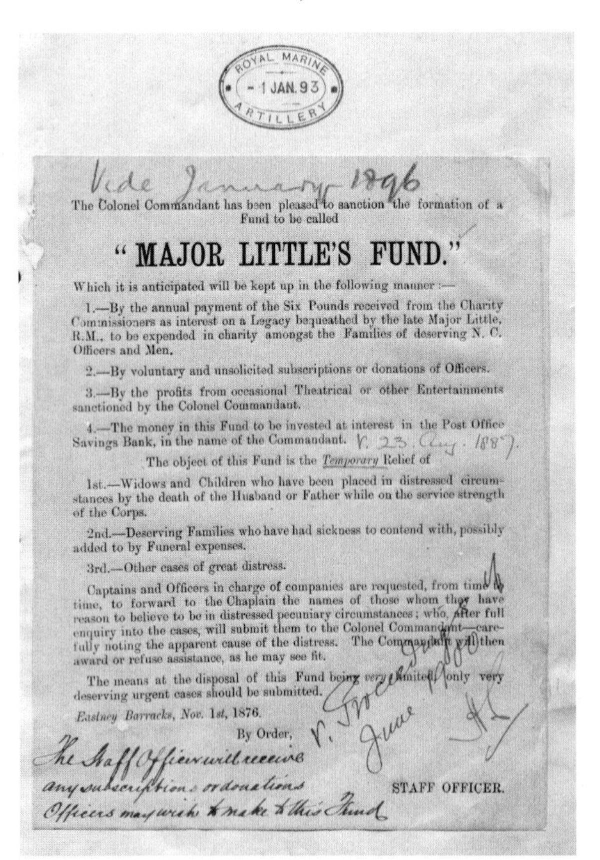

ROYAL MARINE ARTILLERY - 1 JAN. 93

Vide January 1896

The Colonel Commandant has been pleased to sanction the formation of a Fund to be called

"MAJOR LITTLE'S FUND."

Which it is anticipated will be kept up in the following manner:—

1.—By the annual payment of the Six Pounds received from the Charity Commissioners as interest on a Legacy bequeathed by the late Major Little, R.M., to be expended in charity amongst the Families of deserving N. C. Officers and Men.

2.—By voluntary and unsolicited subscriptions or donations of Officers.

3.—By the profits from occasional Theatrical or other Entertainments sanctioned by the Colonel Commandant.

4.—The money in this Fund to be invested at interest in the Post Office Savings Bank, in the name of the Commandant. V. 23. Aug. 1887.

The object of this Fund is the *Temporary* Relief of

1st.—Widows and Children who have been placed in distressed circumstances by the death of the Husband or Father while on the service strength of the Corps.

2nd.—Deserving Families who have had sickness to contend with, possibly added to by Funeral expenses.

3rd.—Other cases of great distress.

Captains and Officers in charge of companies are requested, from time to time, to forward to the Chaplain the names of those whom they have reason to believe to be in distressed pecuniary circumstances; who, after full enquiry into the cases, will submit them to the Colonel Commandant—carefully noting the apparent cause of the distress. The Commandant will then award or refuse assistance, as he may see fit.

The means at the disposal of this Fund being *very* limited, only very deserving urgent cases should be submitted.

Eastney Barracks, Nov. 1st, 1876.

By Order,

STAFF OFFICER.

The Staff Officer will receive any subscriptions or donations Officers may wish to make to this Fund

Notice of Major Little's Fund, 1st November 1876.

Colonel Grover himself had a varied career that typified the versatility of Royal Marines in the twentieth century. He first joined the Army, but at the outbreak of the First World War was commissioned into the Royal Marine Light Infantry in September 1914. He served in RMLI battalions in Gallipoli, Salonica and France from 1915 to 1916, when regular officers were recalled for Sea Service. Upon the award of the First Class Certificate in Gunnery at HMS *Excellent*, he transferred to the RMA, serving aboard HMS *Marlborough*, in the Grand Fleet. The RM 13.5 inch turret was awarded a special plaque for a unique firing record by the gunnery officers of the ship. He also had a short spell as Flight-Lieutenant with the Royal Naval Air Service. After the war he qualified (with a First Class Certificate) as Instructor of Naval Gunnery at HMS *Excellent* and became Adjutant of the RMA Division at Eastney from 1921 until the abolition of the RMA in 1923. After spells in Naval Intelligence he became Instructor of Naval Gunnery, Portsmouth, 1931-34, and finally Director of Naval Recruiting. He was also intensely interested and knowledgeable in Royal Marines history and produced a short history in 1948. He died in 1969 aged seventy-three.

The working day for a Gunner at Eastney, was 6 am to 6 pm with an hour for breakfast, and one and a half hours for dinner in summer, and 8 am to 6 pm with one hour for dinner in winter.

A typical day in 1907 began with reveille at 05.00 and parade at 06.00 for a short march up to Fort Cumberland. After breakfast, all ranks were detailed off for instruction, either in infantry drill and PT on the parade ground, Repository drill at Fort Cumberland, or musketry on the range. In the afternoon, the entire Barracks turned to for fatigues and other unwelcome tasks until 16.30. On Saturday mornings, as a variation, the whole battalion paraded and marched out to an area such as Bedhampton.

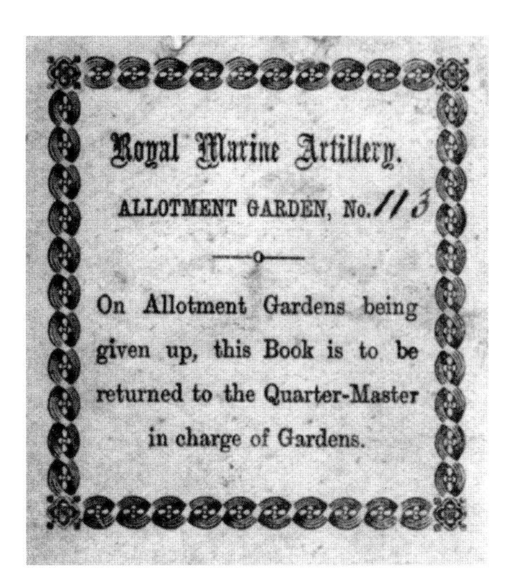

Royal Marine Artillery.

ALLOTMENT GARDEN, No. 113

On Allotment Gardens being given up, this Book is to be returned to the Quarter-Master in charge of Gardens.

Book plate from a book on growing vegetables issued to RMA Gunners who tended allotments.

By 1862, Divisional Standing Orders had stated that the "NCOs in charge of the Cook-houses were to see that the provisions were properly cooked, and that they were to also have charge of the lavatories and baths, and to see them cleaned by the fatigue men every morning". One Private or Gunner was to be employed permanently as a baker, with another detailed to assist in each Cook-house daily up to dinner at 12.30pm. The daily ration per man had been set in 1833 at ¾ lb of meat and 1½ lbs of bread, augmented with any vegetables that could be grown or purchased. Spices and condiments also

Royal Marine Artillery Technical Instruction.

GARDENER.

This is to Certify that Q. M. Sergt Lyne has had considerable experience in "Cottage Gardening" both of Vegetables and Flowers, and has a Good knowledge of this work.

Signed W. Walker Major.

President, R.M.A. Technical Instruction Committee.

Eastney Barracks, Portsmouth, (Date) 20th Sept. 1906.

Certificate for technical Instruction as 'Gardener' for Sergeant George Lyne RMA, 20th September 1906. The gardener would instruct other allotment holders, and inform the Quartermaster when crops were low, so that other vegetables could be purchased elsewhere. Incentives were made to men to tend allotments, as merit points were awarded and displayed in each orderly room. Failure of sufficient merit, and untidiness of an allotment, would result in the plot being divided and half given to the next applicant. These allotments were situated outside the north wall of the Barracks, south of Henderson Road, and by the church and infirmary. Vegetables grown were provided for cook-houses; the men being stopped a half-penny a week from their pay for the produce.

had to be contracted. With breakfast at 7.30 am being the only other official paid meal in the day (and these by way of deductions from pay), men could be left some nineteen hours without food. For those out on the rifle range, lunch was bullock's head soup, sold from a handcart for a penny a mug. If there was any bread left over, this was served at tea at 16.30. To supplement this basic ration the canteen system was developed. 'Wet' (beer) and 'Dry' (grocery) Canteens; businesses run by private merchants under the direction of the Quartermaster, where men could purchase extras such as eggs, tea, bread, butter, milk, tobacco and, of course, beer. The Royal Marine Divisions had regulated the private tenants of the canteens by placing them under the direction of the 1st Quartermaster and a Canteen Committee. A Sergeant was also required to be present during the opening hours. In 1904 the canteen at Eastney was rebuilt and enlarged.

By 1887 a Gunner's pay was a shilling and two-pence a day with a penny beer money. Seven-pence a day was deducted for rations, but in 1904 free bread and meat was introduced and two and a halfpenny's worth of groceries.

In 1887, the clothing issue for NCOs and men consisted of a blue tunic once every two years, a blue kersey jacket, a pair of tweed trousers, a flannel shirt, a pair of boots and a pillbox cap. The kersey was worn for all drills, parades and walking out, except Review Order; the ceremonial inspections, where dress uniform was required.

Eastney Barracks had a boathouse (near left) with direct access to the sea. A team of Gunners hoists a yacht from a bogie prior to it being placed upon supports. The south wing of the Mess can be clearly seen, as can bathing tents on the shore.

The RMA band lead out a detachment from Eastney barracks main gate at Cromwell Road in 1905. The 1863 bell post (see drawing below) can just be seen above the wall in the top left of the photograph.

The daily routine for certain types of officer was in complete contrast to that of the Gunners. In 1889 General Sir George Aston RMA when reminiscing described the system as 'admirable – in fact so good in its way, that to spend more than a year there (Eastney) as a field officer without any responsibility was about as soul-killing an experience as it is possible to devise. Apart from revising my knowledge of drill I don't think my duties could have occupied on average more than about two hours a day. They consisted chiefly of inspecting and sampling bread, and sitting on Boards to survey clothing, equipment and every conceivable sort of store or supply, from a broom-handle to a truss of hay.'

It should be remembered that the men at Eastney were home from sea, and what could appear as a routine or even boring existence was more than made up for by the freedom of dry land, family and friends, and a bed that wasn't a swaying hammock. It was not unusual, during this period, to find an artilleryman's service record recording over half of his term of service being spent afloat. It would be interesting to speculate whether the pace of the march of a detachment leaving Eastney towards the dockyard, lagged behind that of the detachment coming the other way.

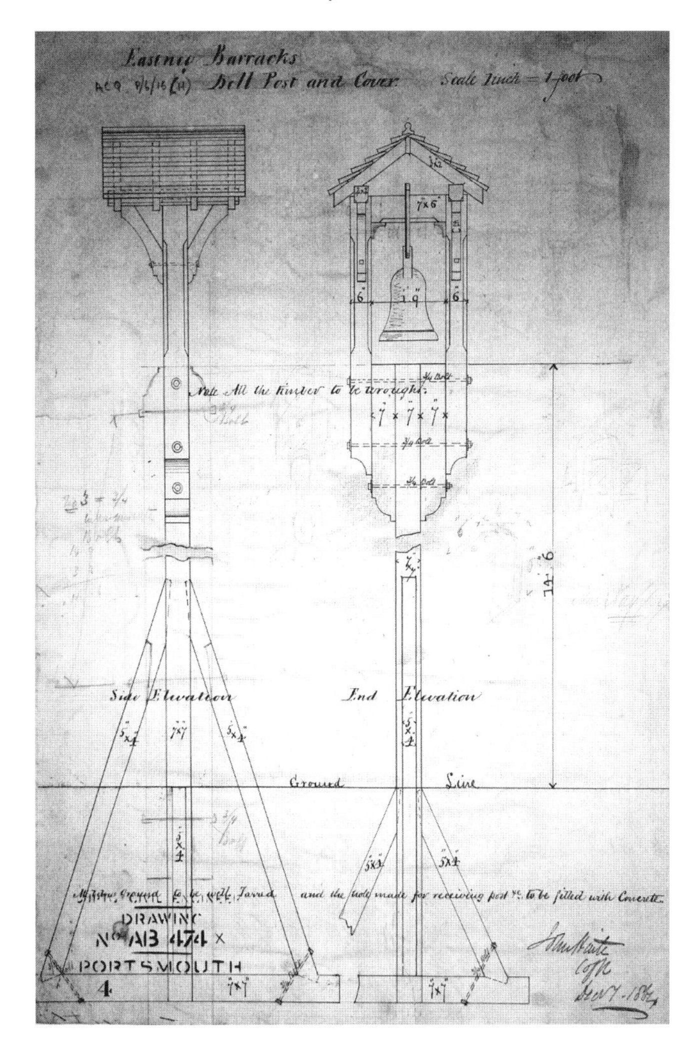

Original drawing of the bell post, 1862. This was located inside the barrack wall at Cromwell Road, north of the entrance. It was used as a fire bell.

6 The Barracks as a Home

ONE OF THE main advantages the Royal Marines had over their Army cousins was their divisional system that afforded them permanent home bases at Chatham, Portsmouth, Plymouth, Woolwich and then Deal. Even though Royal Marines could be recruited from any part of the British Isles, and deploy to ships cruising every sea on the globe, once assigned to a division they would always have a 'home' to return to. An Army regiment on the other hand could be assigned a barracks in a town for a limited duration until either embarking upon campaign, or exchanging with another regiment. For example, a shire name on regimentals was no guarantee of a stay in the county of their title. It was therefore more likely that marines would marry into the city of their division, and a community then to form around their barracks. This was certainly true of Eastney and, being located at an underdeveloped part of Portsea Island, it had exclusive room to do so. Even prior to the full occupation of the barracks, horse-bus services were operated from the dockyard to Eastney and the railway station.

By 1871 there were 1162 servicemen at Eastney, three hundred and six of whom lived outside the barracks. A whole range of trades and services to

The RMA Battalion line the route at the funeral of Queen Victoria who died on the 22nd January 1901.

The RMA detachment for HMS *Exmouth* forming up at E.astney on 5th June 1911.

Ceremonial parade on Southsea Common with the RMA marching past 'at the trail' c.1890.

support the barracks grew outside the walls, with the guarantee of custom from a regular number of inhabitants either departing for, or returning from ships' of the fleet, or land service overseas.

Many local women would be provided with cloth and other materials from the tailor's shop, cut out and ready for them to sew together. On returning with the finished clothing, a fixed price was paid per dozen articles. The shoemaker's shop operated in a similar manner, where boots were

Photograph of W G Blunden, far left; the last shoemaker in the Corps at Eastney. This is likely to have been taken at the closure of the shoemaker's shop (the former sea service battery of 1886) in 1939.

made and repaired by hand, with some work being assigned to the families billeted outside the gates. The shop lasted from 1885 to 1939, after which the work was contracted out to the merchants that had by then established their businesses in the area. As the science of photography became commercially available, photographic businesses began to appear in the area offering the officers and men studio images for their families. With detachments at sea for long commissions, this service became very popular and offered a visible reminder of a husband and father for those left at home.

Apart from the tailor and the shoemaker, the 1905 Standing Orders for the RMA record that there were marines detailed as a carpenter, a blacksmith, a lamplighter, a coal meter, and a store man. Gardeners, armourers, pioneers (general-duty marines), boats crew, schoolmasters and cooks. Civilian nurses, and schoolmistresses were also listed at the barracks.

Studio photograph of an RMA Gunner with a musketry qualification c 1890. The Stobie studio was one of many photographic businesses that established themselves in the area at this time. Note the reference to the Festing Hotel, named after Major Francis Festing RMA.

The RMA fire engine's crew c.1896. The cap tallies read 'RM Artillery' and the crew included a naval 2nd Class Petty Officer. Sergeant James Jefferey RMA (front, third from left) is in charge of the engine.

Advertisement for the Merryweather Fire Escape, as supplied to the RMA Barracks Eastney.

Eastney had schools for boys and men of the Division, and also for the sons and daughters of the marines. The former would employ senior NCOs to improve the literacy of the recruits and Gunners, while the children's school was set up under the Naval Chaplaincy Department. Boys and girls were segregated, with most of the Girls School staffed by civilian teachers. In 1894 they were placed under inspection by the Education Department, to enable them to become eligible for a grant; Portsmouth had by now begun to establish its Corporation schools such as Milton Boys and Girls School in Eastney Road. The 1919 Education Act eventually caused the Admiralty to close the children's schools in the barracks, and those marines on the staff returned to duty. After 1921 only serving marines and musicians received instruction at the school block, and between 1904 and 1905, part of school buildings were converted into married quarters. The remainder was eventually used by the Signal Wing and later became the first home for the Royal Marines Museum in 1958.

Form 9 (A)

Request to get Married.

Years' Service Afloat 2 yrs
No. of Good Conduct Badges 1
Amount in Post Office Bank, £ 5.00
Attested 18th January 1900 Joined Artillery 18th January 1900

M 8664 Co. W. H. Wilkinson R.M. Artillery Barracks, Portsmouth, 9th May 1905 requests the permission of the Commanding Officer to get married to Miss Rhoda Tussler living at Southsea in the Parish of Portsmouth County Hants and is willing to become a member of the Lying-in Fund.

Signature of Applicant W H Wilkinson

I have personally made enquiries & am satisfied as to the respectability of the parties

Approved,

Captain of Company H Worthington Colonel Commandant.

The Officer signing this report is to certify in his own handwriting that he has made enquiries and is satisfied as to the respectability of the parties.

R.M.A. [100] 9/04.

Formal request for permission to marry from Gunner W H Wilkinson RMA signed by Captain Hugo Worthington RMA, 9th May 1905. The annotation is interesting.

From the 1860s NCOs had been billeted with their men in barrack rooms. Married NCOs had the privilege of having their wives live with them in the room. They were normally allocated 'the corner bed-space' and allowed to rig up a canvas screen for privacy, however the ratio permitted for 'live in' wives was 1:100 when space was at a premium. In 1911 the senior NCOs were given separate living quarters in cubicles in C Block of the Main Block.

Men filling palliasses with straw in the Drill Shed at Eastney. The more experienced Gunners would try to compress as much in as possible as this form of mattress would not be refilled for another three months.

Most married NCOs eventually elected to rent rooms or houses outside the barrack walls, and this prompted the growth of streets and public houses around the barracks stretching to Southsea to the west, and Milton village to the north. Many of these streets in Eastney carry the names of Royal Marines, or battles they participated in, such as Festing, Collins, and Adair

Interior shot of a barrack room in the main block at Gunners Walk Eastney c1890. The hoops were originally to hang lamps on but have been converted with gas piping.

Men's barrack room at Eastney. The hand painted crest on the far wall features an anchor, laurel and flaming grenades with a King's Crown, indicating the date as being Edwardian, while the lack of blue home service pattern helmets on the shelves indicate that it is post 1905.

Roads; Kassasin and Tokar Streets, and White Cloud Place after the battle of 1858 in the second China War.

In 1867 Sarah Robinson purchased a plot of land at the junction between what would become Adair Road and Highland Road. She wished to develop a home similar to the Royal Sailor's Rest, except for Royal Marines to spend their time. This became the Victoria Soldiers' Home and, with the Victoria Hall alongside, was opened in 1886. It was enlarged several times, and the hall became the Victoria Wesleyan Church between 1908 and 1911. Eastney Methodist Central Hall which was built in 1928 on the site of the home, was itself demolished and rebuilt in 2003.

Probably like its sister naval ports of Chatham and Plymouth, Portsmouth mythology would claim the city as having the greatest concentration of pubs in the country in the first half of the twentieth century. As Eastney developed around the barracks and its Royal Marines, the pubs would occupy the strategic corners of terrace blocks causing the boundaries of Southsea and Milton to merge with the area to become the south eastern part of the City of Portsmouth. The RMA Tavern, The Eastney Tavern and Eastney Cellars, The Three Marines and Fort Cumberland Arms all still survive at the time of writing; The Barrack Cellar and The Mayflower were demolished in 1972 and 2008 respectively, whilst the Highland Arms, Fort Cumberland Tavern, and The Union Flag, were converted into housing between 1984 and 1991.

Within the barracks, improvements and alterations were not confined to just the training and accommodation of the expanding division; many recreational facilities were also added. The officers' tennis courts had been established in 1878, and La Crosse was introduced by Major F. H. Poore in 1879 and played on the parade. In 1884 a racquet court was built, followed by a bowling alley that was later converted into billiard rooms for the men. In 1890 the wooden floor of the drill shed was replaced by asphalt and soon afterwards a roller skating club was formed.

The men's billiard room at Eastney with the table rules attached to the gas-light piping. Field service caps are worn with duck white jackets by most of the men photographed here.

Ginger beer bottles from the RMA Canteen.

Food and recreation were two of the most vital elements to maintain morale within any military service, and coupled with the educational policy encouraged by the Royal Marines, Colonel Commandants had instructed their Barrackmasters to set up libraries and recreational facilities for the men since the 1840s. The recreation rooms, often adjacent to a seated library and reading room area, contained billiards, bagatelles, dominoes and later skittle alleys. Accompanying both areas was a refreshment bar that eventually was stocked with coffee, soup, ginger beer, bread, ham, cheese, pork pies and Saveloys. Of greater significance were the opening hours up to 10.30 pm, which enabled men to purchase a small supper and supplement the provisions provided by the canteen. Profits from this enterprise, separate from the canteen arrangements, went into sports activities such as the purchase of boots and shirts for the RMA tug-o-war team in the 1890s.

Team sports were further catered for with the creation of football, rugby and cricket pitches on the drill fields, and by the levelling of 'Suther's redoubt'. The land had originally been thirty-three acres of Joliffes Farm, and had been gradually laid down to grass, to be used when ready for drill

Victorian canteen tokens from Eastney Barracks. Items from the canteen were paid for using tokens in an attempt to counter fraud and theft of money. The canteen committee would also set the prices and the value of the tokens.

The construction of the football ground on the field to the rear of the Officers' Mess 1901-2. 'Suther's redoubt' had been levelled, and the ditch filled in to make way for this. Highland House can be seen in the right background.

Officers of the Portsmouth Division, Royal Marines with Captain Gene Tunney USMC (front row in civilian clothes). The World Heavyweight Boxing Champion presented, on behalf of the United States Marine Corps, the Tunney Cup for Corps football during this visit, December 1928. He presented the cup to the Adjutant General, Royal Marines – Major General LST Halliday VC who is seated to Tunney's left in this photograph.

purposes. In 1892 Captain A. L. S. Burrowes RMA became the chief architect for the cricket pitch that, owing to the land being almost at sea level, required 40 tons of chalk from Paulsgrove chalk pit to be laid under the centre. It was ready for matches the following year, and replaced the pitch on Fort Cumberland Glacis which had been used for purely RMA cricket, both among officers and men.

In 1901 the piece of the drill field east of the Officers' Mess was levelled, drained and fenced for a football ground, and after being sown was ready for the 1902-3 season. The cost was £100 and the labour was principally provided in barracks. In 1907 the Sergeants' tennis courts were made, with the Warrant Officers' tennis courts added in 1922. A sports pavilion near the football ground was erected out of the RMA War Memorial Fund (1914-1918), and this was later rebuilt as the Portsmouth Royal Marines Association Club.

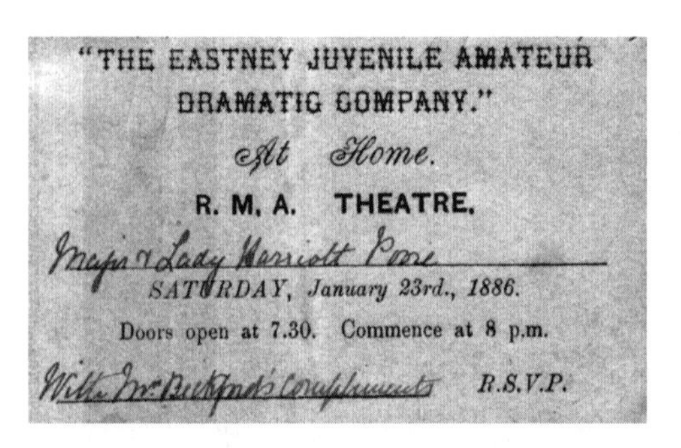

"THE EASTNEY JUVENILE AMATEUR DRAMATIC COMPANY."

At Home.

R. M. A. THEATRE.

Major & Lady Harriott Poore

SATURDAY, January 23rd., 1886.

Doors open at 7.30. Commence at 8 p.m.

R.S.V.P.

Theatre manager's invitation to Major and Lady Harriott Poore for a performance at the original barracks' theatre in 1886.

The RMA built their first theatre in the barracks in 1869; a wooden construction, paid for with money from the canteen funds. Dramatic and variety performances were put on by the talented amongst the division who formed the RMA Theatrical and Variety Companies along with their wives and visiting guest artistes. By 1886 the 'Eastney Juvenile Amateur Dramatic Company' had also been established. In 1899 a new theatre was constructed, later known as the 'Globe Theatre'. The first performance consisted of seventeen variety acts, which included an orchestral band, solo singers, an Indian clubs demonstration, mandolinists, a comedian, a violin soloist, and a dramatic farce. The theatre opened initially only during the winter season, offering entertainment in the form of plays, band and smoking concerts.

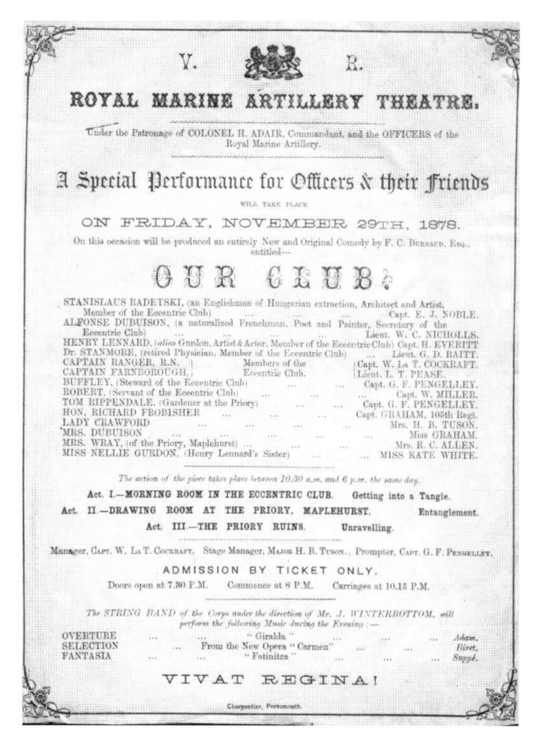

V. R.

ROYAL MARINE ARTILLERY THEATRE.

Under the Patronage of COLONEL H. ADAIR, Commandant, and the OFFICERS of the Royal Marine Artillery.

A Special Performance for Officers & their Friends

WILL TAKE PLACE

ON FRIDAY, NOVEMBER 29TH, 1878.

On this occasion will be produced an entirely New and Original Comedy by F. C. BURNAND, Esq., entitled—

OUR CLUB!

STANISLAUS RADETSKI, (an Englishman of Hungarian extraction, Architect and Artist, Member of the Eccentric Club) ... ... Capt. E. J. NOBLE.
ALFONSE DUBUISON, (a naturalized Frenchman, Poet and Painter, Secretary of the Eccentric Club) ... ... Lieut. W. C. NICHOLLS.
HENRY LENNARD, (*alias* Gurdon, Artist & Actor, Member of the Eccentric Club) Capt. H. EVERITT
Dr. STANMORE, (retired Physician, Member of the Eccentric Club) ... Lieut. G. D. RAITT.
CAPTAIN RANGER, R.N. } Members of the Eccentric Club. { Capt. W. La T. COCKRAFT.
CAPTAIN FARNBOROUGH, } { Lieut. L. T. PEASE.
BUFFLEY, (Steward of the Eccentric Club) ... ... Capt. G. F. PENGELLEY.
ROBERT, (Servant of the Eccentric Club) ... ... Capt. W. MILLER.
TOM RIPPENDALE, (Gardener at the Priory) ... ... Capt. G. F. PENGELLEY.
HON. RICHARD FROBISHER ... ... Capt. GRAHAM, 105th Regt.
LADY CRAWFORD ... ... Mrs. H. B. TUSON.
MRS. DUBUISON ... ... Miss GRAHAM.
MRS. WRAY, (of the Priory, Maplehurst) ... ... Mrs. R. C. ALLEN.
MISS NELLIE GURDON, (Henry Lennard's Sister) ... ... MISS KATE WHITE.

The action of the piece takes place between 10.30 a.m. and 6 p.m. the same day.

Act. I.—MORNING ROOM IN THE ECCENTRIC CLUB. Getting into a Tangle.
Act. II.—DRAWING ROOM AT THE PRIORY, MAPLEHURST. Entanglement.
Act. III.—THE PRIORY RUINS. Unravelling.

Manager, CAPT. W. LA T. COCKRAFT. Stage Manager, MAJOR H. B. TUSON. Prompter, CAPT. G. F. PENGELLEY.

ADMISSION BY TICKET ONLY.

Doors open at 7.30 P.M. Commence at 8 P.M. Carriages at 10.15 P.M.

The STRING BAND of the Corps under the direction of Mr. J. WINTERBOTTOM, will perform the following Music during the Evening:—

OVERTURE ... ... "Giralda" ... ... *Adam.*
SELECTION ... From the New Opera "Carmen" ... ... *Bizet.*
FANTASIA ... ... "Fatinitza" ... ... *Suppé.*

VIVAT REGINA!

Charpentier, Portsmouth.

1878 RMA Theatre bill for the comedy 'Our Club' by F C Burnard. This particular performance featured mainly officers, but many of the shows cast mixtures of officers and men in an environment that seemed acceptable to merge class and rank.

One of these latter concerts was hastily rearranged in the theatre on New Year's Eve 1902 after some of the flimsy Christmas decorations hanging up round the room of the Sergeants' Mess came in contact with the gas, and there was an immediate flare up. Gwendoline Jones, a young sister of Colour Sergeant Jones, RMA who, passing along the road, raised the alarm. Several Sergeants promptly tore down the decorations and trampled out the fire. She was suitably rewarded, and publicly thanked by the Colonel Commandant on the school parade.

In 1904 a benefit night was performed for the retirement of Mrs Cope, a founder member of the Theatrical Company who had never missed a performance in twenty-one years. She was also awarded a miniature Long Service and Good Conduct medal by the Sergeants' Mess! The *Hampshire Telegraph* reported '...Under the direction of Bombardier Beech, part of the band of the corps occupied the orchestra, opening the programme with a neatly played selection. The Blue Marines never forget old faces. True to their favouritism of the past, they accorded a most hearty welcome to Miss Emma Masher, nor was the appreciation of the audience less pronounced when Mr. T J Kerr made an appearance. He has stage managed at the theatre for several seasons, and is most popular with all sections of the corps. Another excellent turn was that of Miss M Foley, whose piano imitations gained for her prolonged applause. This clever young lady is scarcely in her teens, but possesses confidence and ability, which augurs well for her future on the boards. Miss A Smith was encored for a fascinating rendering of "She was a Miller's Daughter," Lieutenant Wace pleased everyone by his banjo-accompanied "Down by the Swanee River," the refrain being taken up with gusto by the crowded house. Other items on the first part of the programme included songs by Lieutenant Twiss, and Mr Charles Watkins,

Colour-Sergeant Sidney Dacombe with his wife and son John (in Cadet uniform). It was popular to sit for a local studio and produce postcards or greetings cards for friends and family. Like many Royal Marines with families, the sons and brothers often followed into the Corps.

Theatre production cast photograph taken in the new 'Globe Theatre', built at Eastney in 1899 to replace the original wooden one. The orchestra pit in the foreground is equipped with electrically lit music stands that would indicate the date as being around 1905.

The cinema at Eastney Barracks which was a conversion of the Globe Theatre built in 1899.

an imitation of bird whistling by Mr W Titheridge, a heavy weightlifting exhibition by Mr S G Dacombe, a display of scientific boxing by Messrs. Hewitt and Lennard, while the gymnastic staff, under QMS Jones, entertained the company to an exhibition of club swinging.'

Lieutenant Hubert Twiss went on to serve with a 4 inch Battery in France in 1915 and was mentioned in despatches, while Sergeant-Major Sidney Dacombe was awarded to Distinguished Conduct Medal at Ypres in 1916 for rescuing three wounded men under fire. His son John ('Jack') became Drum-Major for Portsmouth Divisional Band in the late 1930s. Lieutenant Stephen Wace, went on to be a Major and was awarded a CBE for his work with Wireless Telegraphy on Malta between 1916 and 1919. He died of acute pneumonia in 1920.

By 1921, the theatre was also being used as a cinema, and in 1966 was showing films three times a week. An inspector's report on the redevelopment of Eastney in 1947 had described the theatre as 'a galvanised covered building of inadequate seating capacity, badly planned with poor sight lines; acoustics bad.'

The theatre footlights were improved when electric lighting was installed to Eastney Barracks in 1904. The theatre was eventually pulled down along with the squash court and gymnasium in 1984.

It may seem strange but until the beginning of the twentieth century there had been no official requirement that recruits to the Navy or Royal Marines had to be able to swim. Many obviously could, or would be encouraged to learn, but equally many 'landsmen' were recruited from areas of the country where there was little opportunity, or need, for swimming. Two accidents in one year, of contrasting scale, brought this deficiency into focus. Among deaths recorded in August 1893 by *Globe and Laurel*, were those of a Private Hayes and a Bugler Corponet – both 'drowned whilst bathing' off Eastney. The same edition reported the sinking of HMS *Victoria*, with the loss of 70 lives, after she accidently collided with HMS *Camperdown* on 22nd June during manoeuvres in the Mediterranean. Over the next decade this

Internal view of Eastney swimming pool completed in 1905, and open to the public since 1975.

WINDSOR CASTLE

ROYAL MARINE ARTILLERY SCHOOL,
EASTNEY.

Certificate of Merit

AWARDED TO

Frank W. Crowe

FOR

PROFICIENCY IN SWIMMING.

DISTANCE 40 yds.

Date 25 October 1907

Colonel 2nd Commandant,
President of School Committee.

RMA school swimming certificate for 40 yards in the barracks swimming pool, to Frank Crowe, 25th October 1907.

fundamental skill was addressed by the building of swimming pools at each of the Royal Marines Divisions, as well as naval establishments. Eastney pool was built by Samuel Slater of Yorke Street, Southsea in 1904, being located in a hollow where a natural lake had existed. It measured 68ft by 25ft and was filled with sea water. The walls and base were concrete, 4ft thick; with the flat roof also made of concrete, condensation was so great that spectators wore raincoats. Changing facilities were on the poolside, typical Victorian wooden built individual cubicles with half stable doors. To enable the pool to be emptied and kept dry without the pressure of the surrounding water table rupturing the pool itself, pumps were fitted into three deep wells to lower the level of the water table.

It is unclear when the pool was upgraded and tiled, given a wood lined slate

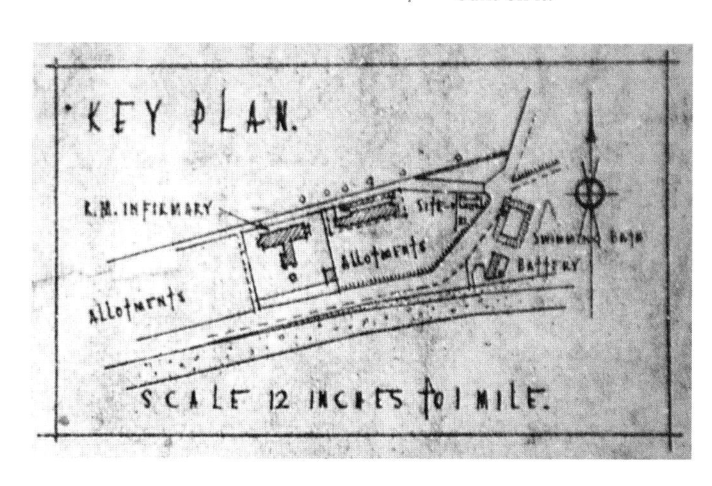

A structural drawing key plan showing the locations of the infirmary, allotments, the swimming pool, and the old coastal sea service battery that in 1939 had a pill-box built on it.

Front cover of the arrivals booklet issued in 1967. Many local shops and services placed advertisements to sponsor its' production.

apex roof and converted to fresh water. The records held by the Department of the Environment where lost or destroyed when the Royal Marines vacated the barracks between 1972-73.

The Royal Marine Artillery Cadets and later the Royal Marines Volunteer Boys Corps (renamed the Royal Marines Volunteer Cadet Corp) where allotted times for swimming on Friday evenings. In 1921 the RMA swimmers test was seven lengths of the pool in a canvas duck suit, while in 1939 Jean Wortham, of Fratton, first went to the pool as a four-year-old when her father was a Royal Marine. 'I used to ride on his back, the pool seemed much bigger then, of course, but the facilities are much the same.'

The booklet issued to new arrivals at Eastney in 1967, gave details of the segregated recreational use of the pool on Fridays 1730-1830 for senior NCOs and families, Saturdays 1300-1500 for other ranks and families, and Sundays 1530-1730 for officers and families.

In 1974 Portsmouth City Council acquired the pool from the Crown agents and set about repairing and modernising for public use. During the refurbishment it was discovered that the boilers were built by dockyard apprentices as test jobs. The two reciprocating pumps were of an unusual type and were made by Messrs Weir & Son of Cathcart. One of these is currently held in Weir's Pump Museum, the other in Eastney Beam Engine House Museum.

The RMA bodyguard to HM King George V at Eastney prior to the voyage aboard HMS *Medina* for the 1911 Delhi Durbar.

The pool opened for public use in 1975 and has undergone further improvements since then. The 2003 World Championship backstroke gold medallist, Katy Sexton had swam at the Eastney pool as a child with a junior group from Portsmouth Northsea Swimming Club in 1990. She recalls 'It was a nice pool to swim in at that age because it's not massive, and when we swam there we would be the only squad in, so it was never overcrowded.'

The officers', NCO's, and men's messes could be regarded as the focal point of the military 'at home,' especially in barracks. By their organisation they defined and divided rank, often class, and then by allocating separate buildings, perpetuated the distinctions.

An Universal Military Dictionary by Captain George Smith in 1779 describes a mess as 'a number of soldiers who, by laying away a certain moiety of their pay towards provisions, mess together. Experience proves that nothing contributes more to the health of a soldier, than a regular and well chosen diet, and his being obliged every day to boil the pot; it corrects drunkenness, and, in great measure, prevents gaming, and thereby desertion.'

Sergeant-Major J Hilson RMA wrote in his diary 'On the 20th May 1866 the sergeants had their first meeting in the Sergeants' Mess at Eastney, and decided to hold on the Queen's birthday, 24th May, a dinner in honour of the occasion. It has proved to be a great boon to us old men, for it has been continued up to the declaration of war (1914), and has given us an opportunity of meeting our old comrades, and of seeing the vast improvements that have taken place. We were now nearly four hundred at Eastney'. In July 1904 a new Sergeants' Mess was opened on the main barrack road leading from the barrack gate at Cromwell Road.

An ensemble from the RMA band performing at a garden party for visiting officers of the Japanese Cruisers *Tsukuba* and *Chitose,* on the 13th July 1907.

Casual group of RMA officers on the steps of the mess at Eastney, with NCOs to the left. Note the original tiled approach to the stairs and the original lamps.

Victorian Soda Syphon, suitably inscribed, from a mess bar at Eastney Barracks.

The mess would also serve as a social reception for visitors either civilian, other services, or on occasion foreign forces. In 1905 the French Navy visited Portsmouth under the 'Entente Cordial', and reciprocal visits to the appropriate messes were entertained. The following year the British-built Japanese battleships *Katori* and *Kashma* visited the port, and Chief Petty Officers visited the RMA Sergeants Mess, whilst the Japanese officers were given a garden party on the lawns in front of the officers mess.

The Officers' Mess building had been completed in 1865, with the dining ante, billiard and library rooms in the centre, and adjoining wings of 'cabins' (single rooms). The mess functioned until 1973, when the contraction of Eastney moved it to the adjacent south wing. Some of the cabins were still used until the closure in 1991.

Before the 1923 amalgamation of the RMA and the RMLI caused an increase in the number of officers at Eastney, only dinner was served in the mess dining room, with all other meals served in the breakfast room. This room was also allocated for Second Lieutenants to take tea, and later a cocktail bar was installed. The other officers had their tea in the ante-room.

The protocol of life in the Officers' Mess required a newly arrived young officer to learn the conventions, customs and traditions quickly in order to be accepted. As senior Majors and Lieutenant Colonels often lived in, they could be intolerant of young officers who did not know their place. Even as late as the 1930s, only reckless young officers dared to approach the carpet in front of the hearth, that was said to be 'strictly reserved for the boots of field officers'. Even taking the only copy of *The Times* was not advisable if there was the slightest chance that some senior officer had not seen it.

Until the mid-1920s the only quarters' furnishings supplied by the Admiralty were fire irons, coal scuttles, Chesterfield tables, Windsor chairs and bedstead mattresses. Floorboards were often bare, and officers would hire furnishings from civilian firms such as Jeeps of High Street, Portsmouth.

There were coal grates in the cabins, but the Officers' Mess at Eastney was regarded by many at this time as a chilly, unwelcoming place. General Blumberg recalls 'the Eastney Mess room used to be the coldest and most uncomfortable room in the kingdom; in the winter the senior officers used to dine in their greatcoats, whilst the rest of us sat and shivered.' In 1947 an official report on the modernization of Eastney Barracks reported 'The Officers' Mess is an example of the Victorian grand manner in planning and design. It is over-large, comfortless, it has a cheerless, repellent atmosphere and arouses but little local enthusiasm.' Such was the post war opinion.

In the early twentieth century the cost of mess living for the junior officer was high, and sometimes beyond the means of their 5/3d a day, pay. In 1918 the daily mess charges were 2/6d for breakfast, 2/6d for lunch, 1/6d for tea and 3/6d for dinner. Full meals cost 10/- a day. Young officers who were unable to afford this expense bought food from the canteen or elsewhere and had their attendants cook it for them. Before 1914, a further cost that had to be met was the provision of livery for the officer's personal batman, and coupled with the cost of his own mess dress, it was not uncommon for officers to build up large mess bills. An Eastney mess tradition arose from the wearing of the pre 1914 ornate RMA mess dress. It was a custom when applauding after dinner to strike the table from underneath because the heavy gold lace in the sleeves would have scratched the polished surface of the table.

In spite of the mess rules and regulations, there were plenty of occasions when a curtain would be temporarily drawn across the bureaucracy and some fun would ensue.

The external stone staircase still bears the scars of previous Guest Night antics when small field guns, kept in the hall, were taken out to the lawns. On one occasion a small car was even man-handled up them for a prank. The internal stairs would not be exempt from the hazards of officers' horse-play either, for despite their grandeur, tobogganing down them on trays was a popular pastime. Major Aston, after returning from the Boer War in 1901, careered down without taking off his spurs; the carpet was cut to threads. A variation on this theme was provided for the officers' children's Christmas

The RMA line the streets during the coronation procession of Edward VII in 1902. The reference to Canada being Britain's 'Granary' sends the message that the Empire is flourishing. Within sixty years it had all but vanished.

Royal Marine Girl Cadet Corps marching on the Main Parade Eastney Barracks, c1934.

parties during the 1950s, when a large chute constructed of white sheets made a slide for the same effect. General Alan Bourne's particular party piece of jumping onto the mantelpiece in the ante-room on Guest Nights was a noteworthy skill given the fireplace (which still survives) is 4 feet 3 inches high. The Padre was not so skilful when demonstrating his golf swing with a walking stick, sending a ball straight into the ante room mirror. However the large mirror, being backed with silver, fetched enough salvage for the pieces to more than pay for the replacement. From hence the new one was known as the 'Padre's Mirror'.

Another aspect of the home life of the barracks was the raising of cadets, usually amongst the children of the men. The RMA Cadets began on 14th February 1901. The *Hampshire Telegraph* reported that it was formed 'with a view to instructing the young generation in drill, discipline, rifle shooting and gymnastics, which all authorities are agreed as being about the most important for ensuring the vigour of the nation'.

They adopted the motto 'Manners Maketh Man', and mustered one hundred and fifty boys by 1902. The uniform was khaki with bandoliers, belts and leggings and a distinctive Veldt slouch hat fashioned after the Boer War headress. The boys, aged between ten and fifteen, met for two hours a week, in the RMA gymnasium in winter and on the drill field in summer. The annual summer camp, held in places like the New Forest, lasted a week. The Cadets were present at the coronation of Edward VII in August 1902 and they were inspected by the Prince of Wales at Eastney in March 1904. By the 1920s they had included civilian children.

Bass Drummer of the RMA Cadet Band c1902. The emblazonment on the drum includes their motto 'Manners Maketh Man'.

The Girl's Ambulance Companies were formed from 1910 at the RM Divisions, and at Eastney there was a RM troop of Girl Guides. In 1927 Mrs A G Little, wife of the Commandant at the time, formed the Royal Marine Girl Cadet Corps. Their standing orders defined their purpose as – 'the inculcation of Discipline, individually and collectively, the improvement of physique and carriage, habits of civility, punctuality, mental and bodily alertness, self-reliance, resourcefulness and comradeship'. It was open only to the daughters of serving or former Royal Marines at a cost of 15/-, and then 2d a week. The uniform was provided. Both of the Cadet units were disbanded and renamed in 1930 as the Roymar Boys and Girls Clubs. This demilitarised modernisation did not remain popular and Girls reverted in 1932. After disbanding during the Second World War, the boys reformed in 1945 with the name Royal Marine Volunteer Cadet Corps.

7 The First World War

THE DECLARATION of war upon Germany on 3rd August 1914 found Britain the only European power without conscription – the armed forces were a profession; you were well trained; you served your king and country; you volunteered.

Fortunately, since 1901 the Admiralty had provided the RFR, the Royal Fleet Reserve, whereby regular Royal Navy and Royal Marines personnel who had completed varying periods of service could be paid to be 'on-call'. Three categories were instigated that allowed for between two months to a years' notice of being recalled. In the case of the Royal Marines this enabled a useful body of NCOs and long service marines to be back at barracks ready to either deploy, or guide and train the influx of recruits and volunteers, many of whom were economical with the truth about their age at this time.

Major General Sir George Grey Aston KCB RMA, had served in Egypt, the Soudan, and South Africa, before becoming Colonel Commandant at Eastney in 1914. He had also been a Professor of Fortification at Greenwich College in 1895, and was the first Royal Marine officer to be a Brigadier General on an Army General Staff (in South Africa).

For the RMA at Eastney, the system appeared to work, but the problem came in the numbers required to man their part of an expanded Grand Fleet. By 1914 the RMA was only 3,393 strong but provided half the detachment strength of the newer *Dreadnought* battleships and battle-cruisers, whilst the RMLI at 13,425 provided the remainder and almost all of the detachments in cruisers and the older warships. The RMA had provided detachments for ships above the class of armoured-cruiser since 1892, but their

The visit of the 1st Lord of the Admiralty, Winston Churchill, to Eastney in 1912; the 13 inch 1855 mortar now serving as a flag staff for the Main Parade.

expertise in power operated turrets drew them in larger numbers to the larger, newer, ships of the fleet.

The primary role of the Royal Marines had always been to provide the fleet's detachments and their share of the naval gunnery, yet a global conflict with simultaneous sea and land operations was going to make greater calls on the manpower. This would result in the RMA requiring to recruit 'short-service' men as the RMLI had, yet the artillery training undertaken at Eastney and Fort Cumberland was more involved than at the other Royal Marine 'infantry' Divisions.

The RMA, being expected to provide land units as part of the RM Brigade, sought to simplify the administration and training of their recruits. In order to keep the training and drafting of the RMA Brigades distinct from the sea service, Sir George Aston, the commandant at Eastney, instituted a Brigade Depot at Fort Cumberland, which trained officers and men in land artillery for the Howitzer and Anti-Aircraft Brigades. From them, men required for coast defences such as the batteries at Cromarty, Scapa, and St Helena, and similar duties were taken. The short-service recruits, after a short course of infantry drill, and a short course of gunnery at the Sea Service Battery, were sent to the Brigade Depot and there trained for the work for which they proved most suitable. Long-service recruits were only instructed in land artillery if detailed for the brigades.

A RM Brigade consisting of three RMLI Battalions and a RMA Battalion served briefly at Ostend from 26th August to 1st September 1914, and then returned to Eastney. All the Marines serving in the RM Brigade at this time were 'long service' men with the exception of the RMA Battalion who had taken sixty of their new short-service recruits to Dunkirk as Motor Drivers. The brigade reformed to return to Belgium, but the RMA Battalion was converted into their specialist Howitzer and AA Brigades, and began training at Fort Cumberland and the barracks.

It was at this time that an unexpected disaster might have developed at Eastney, for on the 15th January 1915, men began to be taken ill. Upon investigation it was discovered that all those sick had come into contact with a visiting Canadian Army football team with whom they had played a match four days earlier. Seven artillerymen died within twenty-one days before it was diagnosed as Cerebro-spinal fever – a disease that had only been identified in England in 1912.

It was probable that fresh and highly virulent strains of the meningococcus were brought to England by the Canadian contingents arriving in the late autumn of 1914. In January 1915, all the known requisite factors for an outbreak of Cerebro-spinal fever were present: severe overcrowding, cold weather, and a population rendered susceptible by youth, by the fatigue of rapid training etc. Recruits have always shared with infants a peculiar susceptibility to what is now known as meningitis. Of the marines who died, only one was older than twenty-one years of age.

Eventually, as the war progressed and casualties mounted, the initial enthusiasm for volunteering waned, and conscription was resorted to. Interestingly, of the new conscripts who were joining, it was noticed at Eastney in October 1916, that many had already seen fighting in France, but had been discharged as under age.

The formation of the RMA Howitzer Brigade came about at the behest of Admiral Sir Reginald Bacon and his connections with the Coventry Ordnance works. Reports of super heavy howitzers used by the Germans at Liège in August 1914, inspired the Admiralty to acquire a dozen 15 inch howitzers, firing a 1,400lb shell. They were the largest 'mobile' howitzer used in the conflict. One was installed at Fort Cumberland for training purposes whilst another remained at Shoeburyness for evaluation: the remaining ten formed into 'one' gun batteries, each with a crew of about eighty-eight men.

Each howitzer dismantled into six separate loads, and to transport the components, ammunition and sundry items required five 100bhp Foster-Daimler tractors and associated trucks. Tractor training was undertaken at the fort with many of the men having been ear-marked from the recruiting process if they had come from agricultural, railway, driving, or mechanised trades. The howitzers suffered various technical problems, the worst being their 11,000 yard range, which required them to be placed much nearer the front line than was desirable for such immobile weapons. The very large shells tended to convert obstructive enemy trenches into large equally obstructive, waterlogged, holes and their blast was too great near friendly infantry.

Their main use was against targets behind enemy lines, such as artillery, observation posts or even whole villages.

The 15 inch howitzers first saw action in France in March 1915, and took part in all the major offensives. One was shipped to Gallipoli, where, true to

A 15 inch howitzer manned by the RMA Howitzer Brigade together with a hall-marked silver howitzer commissioned by the temporary officers of the RMA Howitzer Brigade 1915-1919. This was presented by them to the officers, senior non-commissioned officers and the men of the Royal Marine Artillery and is now on display at the Royal Marines Museum.

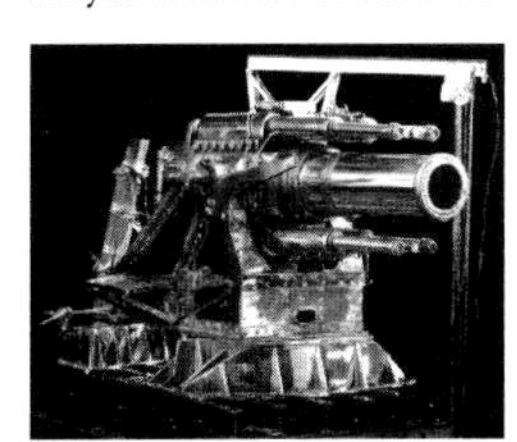

the general planning of that campaign, there was no machinery to unload it. The brigade returned to Eastney for demobilisation in June 1919, minus two guns abandoned and thirty-eight graves in France.

At the other end of the calibre range, the RMA Anti-Aircraft Brigade was formed at Eastney in November 1914, bolting 2 pdr pom-pom guns onto armoured lorries.

3 inch Anti-aircraft gun of the 2nd AA Bde, 1917, showing the gun's crew at drill.

The brigade had four batteries lettered A to D of four guns each. B battery saw action first, in March 1915 near Dunkirk. Anti-aircraft gunnery was an undeveloped science, but the RMA were accustomed to moving targets, and did well with the crude sighting arrangements. Aircraft flying low at this time could do infinite damage by machine gun fire, or by accurate dropping of their bombs, while the fire of the anti-aircraft guns could only effectively keep them at a height that would impair this accuracy: the cost being a considerable expenditure of ammunition. Three of the batteries were eventually absorbed into the Royal Artillery, leaving B battery to re-equip with converted field guns and 3 inch high angle guns. The battery fired its last shots in October 1918, returning to Eastney the following January.

Other RMA units were formed at Eastney and Fort Cumberland in addition to those mentioned and the ships' detachments of the fleet. These included:-

- Gunnery Instructors for Defensively Armed Merchant Ships (DAMS)
- A small detachment landed at Gallipoli in May 1915 using Japanese mortar-howitzers (27lb shells) until other guns arrived.
- A battery for German SW Africa used guns from Malta garrison; 12 pdrs and 4 inch naval guns. This was added to by reinforcements from Eastney with five different types of guns and ammunition scrounged from

The RMA instructional team sent to German South-West Africa where they formed the nucleus of the South African Heavy Artillery.

obsolete weapons not destined for France. Old Boer War 4.7 inch guns were also used. RMA personnel served with 71st Siege Battery, South African Heavy Artillery

- The 4.7 inch guns used by RMA in Serbia, were lost at the fall of Belgrade.
- A battery of 6 inch guns was manned by RMA personnel in Salonika.
- Two officers and fifty-one men were deployed with 4th Battalion for the Zeebrugge Raid of 23rd April 1918. One 11 inch howitzer, four Stokes guns, two 7.5 inch howitzers, five 2 pdr pom- poms, and sixteen Lewis guns were manned aboard HMS *Vindictive*
- The RMA took over RN Heavy Siege Train from 1916 to 1918 in France and Belgium, and manned 9.2 inch and 12 inch guns. Both these gun types were trained on at the sea-service battery at Eastney.
- The RMA provided 12 pdr batteries for the North Russia Field Force 1918-19, in the allied campaign against the Bolsheviks.

Officers and men of the RMA Siege Regiment with their steam tractors at Fort Cumberland.

The return to Eastney Barracks of the officers and men of the RMA Siege Regiment who had served in East Africa during 1916 and 1917.

The Museum's Garden of Remembrance with, in the forefront, the memorial to Brigadier General F W Lumsden VC CB DSO***. He was also Mentioned in Despatches four times.

By the end of the war the strength of the Royal Marine Artillery stood at 7,947 with casualties of six hundred and ninety dead and four hundred and thirty six wounded. In addition to various memorials, the RMA placed oak boards, with the names of those who died, in the Drill Shed at Eastney. When the shed was demolished in the 1990s the boards were remounted in the lower entrance to the RM Museum.

8 Between the Wars

THE ELATION of the Armistice of the 11th November 1918 was not followed by an instant return to peace, or a return home for the RMA units to Eastney or Fort Cumberland. The time taken to demobilise ran far into 1919, and personnel were further committed to the Russian Civil War, the Grecian –Turkish troubles following the capitulation of Turkey, and closer to home, Ireland in 1920. Those that were not discharged into a far from comfortable victorious Britain outside the barracks gates, carried on as before. Gunner Breeze RMA wrote of the new battle-cruiser HMS *Hood*:- 'We were at Eastney, training at Fort Cumberland and the Gunnery school, and some of us were given an extra course and sent to HMS *Glorious* where we trained on a single 15 inch gun turret which was the nearest to the Class C guns aboard the *Hood*, in March 1920. It was in April 1920 that the Sergeant Major came into the barrack room and said 'Gunner Breeze you are on draft to the *Hood*'. Ever after that I was known as Windy'.

The close knit community of the barracks and the surrounding area was mirrored by the family connections within the Corps, or the Navy; Harold 'Taffy' Lewis recorded the following:-

'I went to school in Eastney Barracks, as did most of the children who lived in houses adjacent to the barracks. Only children whose fathers were serving in the armed forces were allowed to go to the Barrack School. My father was in the Royal Navy but my mother's family were all Royal Marine Artillery as it was then.

'I was born in Worsley Street near enough to the sea to hear the waves lapping on shingle on still, winter nights. The houses were small two up and two down and a scullery, with the privvy at the bottom of the garden, but we all seemed quite content and the rent was only four shillings a week (20p). In rough weather and at high tide the sea would come right up St Georges Road and I remember one winter it came up outside our door and the boys were fishing out of the bedroom windows with a bent pin and piece of string.

'I decided to become a Marine because it was better than being a farm labourer. My uncle was a Marine also. Because my name is Lewis they said

I was a "Taffy". My home was Pimlico, a village in Northants not Wales, but the name stuck. I joined in 1921 when we were the Royal Marine Light Infantry, the Red Marines. All in all it was a good life because I stayed 25 years. I lived in Eastney Barracks from time to time. I served on several ships – The *Iron Duke*, *Warspite, Royal Oak*, *Barham* and others. As befitting a Marine, I learnt a lot about guns, eventually becoming an armourer. For two years I was a gunnery instructor at Fort Cumberland.'

Perhaps the most significant event to face the Royal Marines in Portsmouth after the First World War was the amalgamation of the Royal Marine Artillery and the Royal Marine Light Infantry into a single corps. This had been under consideration since 1919, when demobilisation reduced the Corps strength from fifty-five thousand to fifteen thousand. By 1922, the Treasury, after attempting to save expenditure and abolish the Royal Marines altogether, reduced their number to nine thousand five hundred on the understanding that one division was to be given up. The other factors influencing the decision were -

- the similarity of training in naval gunnery
- similarity of employment on board ship
- equalising of pay of RMA and RMLI

These factors spelt out the end for the RMA as a separate body which ever division was lost, but having effectively two divisions of Royal Marines within ten miles of each other seemed to indicate that either Eastney or Forton would be at least the most economic choice. In the event, the alternative option of closing the 'First' RM Division, Chatham, was historically unpalatable to the Corps, although saving it only prolonged its life for a further twenty-seven years.

The amalgamation took effect from 22nd June, 1923, and it was the red tunics of Portsmouth Division RMLI who marched out of Forton and into Eastney on 1st August.

There had always been some rivalry between the two branches of the Corps with the Royal Marine Artillery considering themselves as rather superior. Indeed a story concerning one young man, whose forebears had always been in the RMA, had not passed high enough to get in, but had instead accepted a commission in the Royal Marine Light Infantry. His father had, as a result, refused to give him anything but the minimum compulsory allowance until the amalgamation, when he relented! For the Gunners at Eastney it was not just pride at stake; there was expressed, in some rooms, a sense of their home being invaded, and it was reported that some of the infantrymen were spat at and jeered rather than cheered, as they entered the barracks.

The Admiralty, perhaps having been made quietly aware of potential friction had set about fashioning a unifying speech for King George V to address the 'new' Royal Marines. They also took the opportunity to slope any responsibility for the reduction by planting the words 'financial

The first parade after the amalgamation of the Royal Marine Artillery with the Royal Marine Light Infantry. Eastney Barracks, now the home of the Portsmouth Division, Royal Marines, 1923.

economies' within the announcement, thus placing any wrath at the door of the Treasury. Much was made of it 'being only a reversion to the proud title of a hundred years before' while replacing the ranks of Gunner and Private with that of Marine. They were also careful to badge and uniform the new Corps with combinations of the previous attire. The blue tunic of the RMA was retained, but the cording was replaced by the slashed cuff which had been such a distinguished feature of the RMLI coat, and the officers and Sergeants now wore the infantry sash. Grenade and bugle were replaced by the Corps Crest, and the infantry stripe was adopted on the trousers.

Undoubtedly scarlet was easily damaged by boat work, but the officers wore the scarlet mess-jacket. Blue and khaki are used for working kit according to the nature of employment. In this way the Royal Marines evolved an entirely distinctive uniform.

A cadre of officers and NCOs would continue to be trained at the School of Land Artillery in Fort Cumberland, and the Small Arms School went to Browndown near Gosport, but otherwise the training of the division would be as infantrymen and seaman gunners, with Deal chosen as the centralised recruit training establishment.

The Corps needed a new role, and the official instructions read:-

> 'Its function in war and peace is to provide detachments which, whilst fully capable of manning their share of the gun armament of ships, are specially trained to provide a striking force, drawn either from the Divisions or from the Fleet. These are to be immediately available for use under the direction of the Commander-in-Chief for amphibious operations such as raids on the enemy coastline and bases, or the seizure and defence of temporary bases for the use of our own Fleet.'

The first two elements of this role were familiar ground to the now combined branches of the Royal Marines; the amphibious element would require some updating and development.

During the 1920s one, possibly more, of the casements was converted to a workshop equipped with lathes, grinders etc. Power was provided by a petrol engine complete with radiator cooling system, and the power was transferred through a lay-shaft and belting system – as commonly used in factories at that time. To support the lay-shaft the marines used the skills gained through gantry and pier construction.

Fort Cumberland was the test bed for this work, having become the RMA Anti-Aircraft and Coastal and Naval Bombardment Training Base in 1919. In the autumn of 1923 the sinister sounding 'X' Organisation was formed. Fort Cumberland itself would need a little updating to accommodate the work of its new occupants, and although some lines of electricity and telephone had been supplied in 1905, the *Globe and Laurel* for 1928 printed the following;-

'Just when British trade is showing signs of recovery, a deadly thrust has been aimed at the Lamp and Candle Industries by the Portsmouth Works Department, who have laid an electric lighting cable up to the outside of Fort Cumberland. From what we know of such matters, the threatened industries will have plenty of time to ask questions in Parliament before any fruit in the shape of electric light bulbs sprouts on the possible extension inside the Fort. It is also not unlikely that the society for the Preservation of England's Beauty Spots may object to any tampering with this fascinating glimpse of Old England'. The cabling referred to was more likely to have been for the increased power required for the workshop and industrial machinery that was going to need to be installed.

Original casements, later used as workshops, in 2008.

Although slightly blurred this aerial photograph (c.1926) clearly shows the geometry of Fort Cumberland and illustrates its suitability for the trials and training that took place upon, around, over and in it. The entrance to Langstone Harbour, the ferry terminals and the road built to bypass the musketry ranges are also visible.

The Emergency Sea-Plane Base. In 1928 a trial was carried out into the use of the Fort Cumberland area as an emergency seaplane base. No doubt the facilities at the Fort, combined with a sheltered location, led to this. A wooden ramp, to be laid across the shore to protect the floats and to enable the seaplane to be taken out of the water, was required a) This was constructed on the ramp of the Central Bastion of Fort Cumberland. When complete a lorry was driven down the ramp, presumably to test its strength. b) With the ramp in position officers and men await the arrival of the seaplane. Note that some men are wearing deep wading oilskins. c) During his approach the pilot takes a photograph of the entrance to Langstone Harbour. Details are later recorded on the print as '10 Group B627 P. Emergency Seaplane Base 19.6.28 1200 F6 800'. The photograph clearly shows the ramp over the beach area. The spoil heap adjacent to the ramp is from the sewerage tank excavations. In the background can be seen Eastney Lake and the road constructed by the RMA to allow traffic to bypass the ranges which are also clearly visible within the encircling road. The entire area is pockmarked with excavations and tracks showing how heavily the area was used for trials and training. The large block adjacent to Ferry Road on the shore of Eastney Lake is an observation platform built to enable trials and exercises to be viewed. d) Upon landing the seaplane taxis carefully towards the ramp. The seaplane is a Fairey F111, an aircraft that was in service with the Fleet Air Arm since it was formed in 1923. e) The pilot chats to one of the watching officers as his aircraft his pulled up the ramp.

f) The seaplane is carefully hauled from the sea on its bogie under the watchful eye of the pilot who, wearing his flying helmet, stands on the ramp in front of the aircraft. g) At the top of the ramp the seaplane is carefully rotated on the bogie. Hauling cables, used to tow the aircraft up the ramp by a tractor, are also visible. On the right of the picture the pilot can be seen talking to a RM officer. Above them can be seen the Eastney ferry buildings. The men manoeuvring the tail are wearing the waders and, just below the tail, in the distance, the large observation platform can be seen. h) The seaplane at the top of the ramp. i) The seaplane is carefully lowered down the ramp. The pilot is in his cockpit and marines are also on the aircraft – possibly in an effort to balance the aircraft as it is manouvred over the 'hump' of the ramp. j) At the top of the ramp the aircraft is turned, using the bogie, to face the water. k) Successfully re-launched the seaplane gathers speed as it prepares to take-off. l) With the trial complete the officers and men make their way off the shore. In the background can be seen the steam driven earth-mover working on the installation of the sewerage system, the spoil heap, ventilation shaft and outfall pier.

The 'X' Organisation experimented with methods of landing guns etc. over scaffolding piers 'mainly by extemporisation, brute force and guts'. The unit also experimented with coast and AA gunnery, 4 inch and 6 inch gun repository, searchlight and sound locator training, surveying, motor transport and a mobile workshop. In one exercise in the summer of 1934 Dumaresq fire control tables, of the type used by RM Musicians in warships, were transported and set up with range finders in addition to the usual guns and mounts. A garage and motor transport shed were built within the fort to house the experimental towing vehicles, and by 1930 most of the fort's defensive guns had been dismounted or cut up. In 1935 the fort was designated a 'School of Land Artillery'. The organisation became the basis of the wartime Mobile Naval Base Defence Organisation (MNBDO). After a major exercise in 1935 on the Isle of Arran (Scotland), the unit arrived in Alexandria on 23 September, worked on defences in Egypt and Palestine, and returned to Britain in July 1936.

Wharf gantry trials at Fort Cumberland. Gantry has been erected on top of the Fort walls to give the effect of unloading from ship or barge in harbour. A heavy gun barrel is being lifted prior to being turned and run back beneath the gantry.

The authorised strength was then increased, but men were drafted from the unit in 1938 to bring fleet detachments up to war-strength.

The other unit that joined them was the Inter Service Technical Development Centre. In 1935 the Imperial Defence College, all three Staff Colleges and the Directorate of Sea Transport recommended the establishment of the ISTDC to investigate the theory, method, material, and tactics required to conduct opposed landings on enemy coasts, amongst other agenda. In July 1938 the centre was set up at Fort Cumberland where its proximity to the RM barracks was an advantage, as the latter were always willing to help in experiments and the provision of personnel and equipment. The ISTDC consisted of a Captain RN, (Commandant), a Major, a Wing Commander and a Captain RM (Adjutant). Its terms of reference were to study the development of material, technique and tactics for all Inter-Services

As artillery developed so more trials and experiments were necessary in order to devise suitable 'lifting and shifting' procedures. This picture, taken in 1934, shows the mounting for an anti-aircraft gun being lifted from a lorry onto the ramparts of Fort Cumberland. The load weighs 7.5 tons and is 6 metres long and 2.5 metres high. This was part of the installation of pom-pom and multiple machine gun defences on the south-east bastion of the Fort.

Stacked material for pier and gantry trials and training was stored, maintained and prepared at Fort Cumberland. Here, stores have been accumulated for a forthcoming exercise or trial. The land, very close to the ferry point, is scarred by continual use and tracks used for bringing guns and equipment ashore are easily seen. The Hayling Island ferry landing stage is in the background.

The end result of the accumulation of material is a completed pier and gantry. An 8 inch breech loading gun is being lifted from a barge. A Hathi tractor and gun transporter has been reversed onto the pier making the total weight on the pier 18 tons. Royal Marines designed the pier and then built it in 12.5 hours without any mechanical means of lifting to assist them.

operations. In August, 1938, the ISTDC submitted an interim report in which the main recommendations concerned with combined operations were:

1. A landing craft carrier should be provided by the Admiralty.
2. Designs should be prepared for a self-propelled assault landing craft to carry a platoon of infantry at 8-10 knots and to have a low silhouette so as to attain some surprise.
3. Experiments should be carried out with beach piers over which to discharge stores.

In response, orders were given for one self-propelled landing craft to be constructed. It recommended that the ISTDC should investigate the use of infra-red rays for beach finding; the problems of naval gunfire in support

Left: 'Table Fire Director No 3'. This type of gun direction equipment had been used by Royal Marine Musicians working in ships transmitting stations since World War I. Just prior to the Second World War similar equipment began to appear in association with land artillery.

Right: The delicate transmitting stations were housed in protected Nissen huts.

Demonstration for senior officers of a 6 inch howitzer being hauled through Portsmouth Canal

Tractor trials take place on the spit of land between Fort Cumberland and the ferry, and adjacent to Ferry Road and the Eastney Lake. The specially constructed observation platform is in the background.

Height and range-finder type UBIIA, used in conjunction with 6 inch guns, showing the crew positions. By this time, during the Second World War, gunnery was becoming ever more technical.

of the Army; and of the beach piers for the discharge of stores. The work however, was temporarily interrupted, and when it resumed the next year, activities were restricted to a few Landing Craft Assault, Mechanised, and one Landing Craft Support being constructed and trialled.

The minutes of the meetings of the Chiefs of Staff in December, 1938, reveal the trend of thought at that time:—

'The Admiralty could not visualise any particular combined operation taking place, and were not, therefore, prepared to devote any considerable

a)
b)
c)
d)
e)
E9
f)
MLC
E9

The Development of Landing Craft at Eastney. Before the establishment of the Inter Service Technical Development Centre at Fort Cumberland in 1938, much development work, based upon the lessons learnt during World War I, took place. Mechanised Landing Craft (MLC) were designed and MLCs 1-9 were used as test-beds for the propulsion units. MLC10 was the first landing craft of its type and was brought to Eastney for disembarkation and embarkation trials in 1929. a) MLC10 in Langstone Harbour, October 1929. b) MLC10 cautiously makes her way towards the Eastney beach. Hayling Island shoreline is in the background. c) June 1930, MLC10 after modification. In very inclement weather, light tank T197 disembarks from her. d) On this occasion the landing craft is carrying two tanks. e) These trials continued at Eastney with different vehicles until September 1930. f) Possibly taken in September 1930 this picture shows a Mk II Light Tank coming ashore. One of the landing craft's bow stabilizers can be clearly seen in its extended position in this view – as can the ferry buildings on Hayling Island. g) Disembarkation trials with a Mk II Light Tank. A 'shallow plunge' – the tank lands in 45cms of water. h) A 'deep plunge', landing onto soft sand in water having a depth of 1.3metres. i) The Mk II tank makes its way ashore over soft sand j) – but fails to negotiate the mud and reach dry land. The soft sand/mud and the horizons would indicate that this trial took place to the north of Fort Cumberland, probably adjacent to Ferry Road. k) Gantry built on the foreshore for loading/unloading trials with MLC10 and the Light Tank. 2nd June 1932.

sum of money to equipment for combined training. In any case, only a limited amount of expenditure could be justified in peace time.'

However, General Ismay commented 'We should be making poor use of our strong suit, command of the sea, if we relegated Combined Operations to the background of our war plans.'

Nevertheless, it was agreed that the cost of providing the small quantity of material for the ISTDC should be shared equally between the three Services.

A list of the more important subjects being studied at ISTDC in early 1939 gives some idea of the work of the centre and how much of it was to be attempted by MNBDO, and later used by the Royal Marines in general.

- Dropping troops by parachute.
- Landing water and petrol in amphibious operations.
- Landing tanks.
- Use of amphibian tanks.
- Methods of crossing underwater obstacles.
- Maintenance and supply from the air.
- Use of ships as headquarters for amphibious operations.
- Production of a floating pier.
- Provision of landing punts for coastal raids.
- Design of a tank landing craft.
- Beach organisation.
- Beach roadways.
- Floating piers.
- Transport of troops by air.

Although often referred to as a tough life, joining the services – as it had been in the past – provided a job, living, food, clothing, and a roof. The Royal Marines were perhaps offered the best of both worlds in their established barracks, and their travels with the Navy. With the depression of the 1930s men elected to join as regulars, even when it seemed war could be approaching.

Bernard Fountain recalls when he joined up:

'The chap in charge at that time was RSM F V Burrett, and one of his claims to fame, I should think, was that he had the loudest voice I've ever heard of anybody. And I understand that on one occasion to settle a bet in the Officers' Mess he did in fact stand on the balcony on the roof of the mess and drill the squad in Fort Cumberland'.

c.1930. A parade for inspection takes place on the old Recruits Parade Ground.

In 1938 Frank Agass described the daily routine at Eastney as -

'Breakfast was at seven, between six and seven you got up, washed, shaved – if you were old enough to shave in those days – cleaned the barrack room and then prepared yourself for the first parade which was at five minutes to eight ... five minutes to eight the bugle called ... We then drilled and learnt many various aspects of our weapons... learnt to put pieces of our equipment together. We were taught how to blanco our gear, how to clean it and generally look after ourselves ... [lunch] 12 o'clock ... same routine, PT or football or something else in the afternoon ... By the time you'd finished cleaning your gear at night, cleaned all your brasses, making sure your boots were clean you were ready to go to sleep ... in the main drill shed there was what you called the UAF, which consisted of four billiard tables and a reading room where I discovered for the first time in my life the comfort of an armchair, which I had never had at home, and they were beautifully-upholstered leather armchairs, and the library was very well stocked and there was newspapers every day.'

The King's Birthday Parade 1934, Southsea Common. The Saluting Battery was part of 3.7 inch Howitzer Battery, Royal Marines. The Battery Commander was Captain J H G Wills RM with Lieutenants H D Fellowes and C S Watson.

On the 30th June 1936 Edward VIII made his first and only visit to Eastney, indeed it was the first time a reigning monarch had been on Parade at the barracks. The battalion, band and 241 and 242 Recruit Squads were duly inspected. Interestingly, accompanying him that day were Admiral Roger Keyes, Lord Louis Mountbatten, and Brigadier Alan Bourne RM. These three men would some six years later be wrestling the Corps into Combined Operations and the Commando role. For the King, he wrestled with his conscience for a further six months and abdicated on the 11th December: he was never crowned.

King Edward VIII is seen leaving the saluting base during his visit to Eastney Barracks in 1936.

9 The Second World War

THE AUGUST of 1939 brought an influx of Royal Marines back through the barrack's gates; regulars awaiting assignments to the turrets aboard Royal Navy ships, pensioners recalled to train, or administer the paperwork or serve aboard DEMS (Defensively Equipped Merchant Ships, or 'don't ever mention ships' as they were sarcastically called). 'HOs' (Hostility Only) officers and men, volunteers and called-up men, added to the activity. To cope with the influx of new recruits, the well-tended allotments behind St Andrew's Church were flattened and Nissen huts built on top of them in October 1939. This became known as Hutment Camp.

Concrete machine gun pill-boxes were sunk into earthworks in both Eastney Fort East and West. Another was placed adjacent to the barracks swimming pool on the site of the old practise battery, to command a field of

Inside the Machine Gun Lecture Room at the Gunnery School, Royal Marines, a Royal Marine Instructor teaches Royal Navy DEMS Gunners. (Defensively Equipped Merchant Ships)

fire across the now barbed wired beach. Blast shelters were also erected along the length of Gunners Walk next to the parade ground, yet other preparations seemed curiously at odds with this strategy. The influx of young officers required further accommodation which resulted in a highly exposed flimsy wooden 'shack' being constructed in front of the parade ground bank, while a lone .303 inch Lewis gun was mounted at the flag staff on top of the clock tower. A young Probationary 2nd Lieutenant Ian Gourlay (later Major General) was tasked with counting, daily, the expenditure of ammunition of this weapon from the poor 'vertigo free' marine who had to man it. What this single gun was to achieve against any Luftwaffe plane flying at over two hundred and fifty miles an hour was anyone's guess.

Likewise when war was declared on 3 September 1939 and the Orderly Officer reported the news to the senior officer in the mess requesting his orders, the reply was an unexcitable 'Shut the White Gate.' This gate enabled officers access to the barracks behind Eastney Fort West and along the front of Teapot Row. Eastney had prepared its defences.

For new Royal Marines, a camp at Exton in Devon was already being constructed and its first intended inmates assembled at Eastney Barracks as the 'RM Special Reserve' on 12 October. They were under the care of Major G W M Grover RM , whilst the Commanding Officer, Lt Colonel C R W Lamplough RM was detained on urgent work at the Admiralty. The first two hundred and fifty recruits soon swelled to four hundred undertaking a six weeks disciplinary course (HO 1-10 Squads) which they completed by the end of November. The majority of these men were assigned to the Mobile Naval Base Defence Organisation for Anti Aircraft Artillery, whilst their still warm beds were quickly filled by the second four hundred (HO 11-20 Squads) who occupied them until 26 January 1940. The first six of these squads also went to the Mobile Naval Base Defence Organisation and the other four remained at Eastney to form part of the RM Brigade. One man from this entry achieved notoriety as 'the Marine who never was',

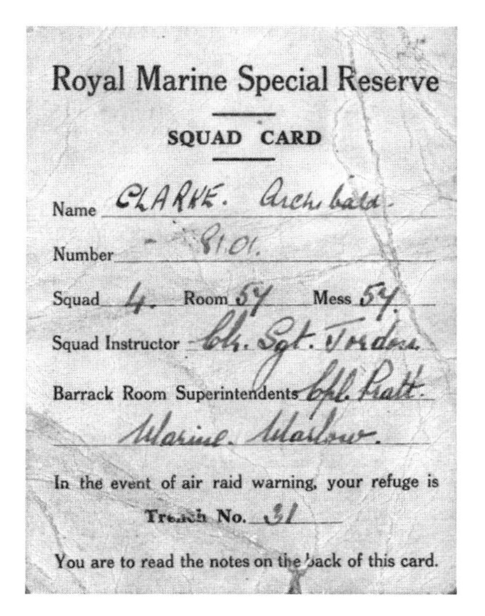

Royal Marine Special Reserve

SQUAD CARD

Name CLARKE. Archibald.

Number 9101.

Squad 4. Room 54 Mess 54.

Squad Instructor Ch. Sgt. Jordan.

Barrack Room Superintendents Cpl. Pratt. Marine Marlow.

In the event of air raid warning, your refuge is

Trench No. 31

You are to read the notes on the back of this card.

INSTRUCTIONS

EASTNEY 10/10/39

Don't lose this card.

You should pass through the following departments:—
Medical (inspection by medical officer).
Dental (" " dental ").
1st Quartermaster (for issue of clothing).
Anti-gas (for issue of anti-gas respirator).
Gas chamber (to test your respirator).

You should have filled up your next of kin form.

You should have writen home on the postcard provided.

You should see that all your kit is clearly marked with your number.

You will visit the Pay Office to-morrow to make any allotment you may wish, to your relations.

If you want to know anything, please ask your squad instructor or anyone in authority.

We are all out to help you.

Barrack card, front and back, issued on the outbreak of war, 1939.

for a Marine Murray reported sick on the day of joining at Eastney, was rushed to Haslar Hospital for an emergency operation and thence discharged without ever having been in uniform or sleeping in a barrack bed!

The experience of being a new recruit at Eastney during the war is recalled by Marine Archibald Clarke who arrived at the barracks entrance in Cromwell Road on 10th October 1939.

'The entrance was imposing – a wide gateway, heavy studded wooden gates opened inwards and secured by large steel bolts let into the ground. On each side stone pillars rose to support a magnificent ornamental arch set into a tall thick wall topped by three strands of barbed wire, which stretched for several hundred yards before curving out of view. A large sign announced that this was Eastney Barracks, and a large sergeant moved from the centre of the gateway to allow the lorry to enter.

'In the drill shed, ten squads of forty men could drill at the same time, and in bad weather the crash of eight hundred army boots meeting concrete was deafening. With ten instructors' voices echoing from the roof as they tried to avoid collisions, everyone listening acutely but not always hearing the order meant for them, proceedings sometimes lapsed into pure farce. Once a quarter of our squad turned right and the remainder marched on. Colour Sergeant Jordan surveyed the resultant chaos sorrowfully. "O'Grady says we made a right cock-up of that", he said succinctly. The drill shed was now being used as a reception centre. Tables had been set up and here we reported in, were given Corps, Room and Squad number, then guided to the Recruit Block. This had its own parade ground. A prison like building of four storeys, the ground floor housed toilets, bath and washrooms. All the rooms in the barracks were of the same pattern and size. High white ceilings, green walls, brown lino on the floors. In the centre of the room a pot bellied stove stood on a steel-plated area. Cast into one of the iron walls of the coal bunker was the regimental crest and the date – 1867. There were probably more than twenty men living in the room then, but the solid iron beds, with palisades (sic) on woven steel bases, could have been the original ones. A long rifle rack in the centre of the room and a wooden shelf over each bed completed the furniture. The next day, after being roused at 6.00 by three buglers blasting reveille in unison under our windows, and after our first meal, we were taken on a tour of inspection. At the sick bay, we received our first injection and a short lecture from the doctor on the perils of mixing with those horrible civvies on the other side of that wall. As we were all still dressed in civilian clothes, it got rather a gruesome lecture off on a light-hearted note.

'We skirted the sports field, two football and one rugby pitch laid out, then stopped at the detention quarters – a rather dark interior as all windows were high, small and barred. A central gangway served six small cells on either side. White painted walls, concrete floor, bed and blankets, rather spartan but warm and not so different from the barrack rooms.

'On the way back we passed the large gymnasium and the theatre which doubled as a lecture room. I found later that this building had comfortable seating, a good stage and was able to seat several hundred people. Our morning walk ended outside the dining hall in time for lunch. We had now been briefly introduced to our home for the next two months, to which those of us who were lucky would return at intervals over the next six years.'

Marine Clarke's reference to luck was poignant, as four days after he entered the barracks as a recruit, ninety-two regulars from the barracks were killed as the Portsmouth based battleship HMS *Royal Oak* was torpedoed at anchor in Scapa Flow by U-47. Not for the last time, the names of those lost were pinned to the notice board outside the barrack wall.

Harry Gould volunteered for the Royal Marines and made a few notes in his diary at the time:-

'arrived at Eastney Barracks 9.30am August 7th, 1940.
Swimming, 12 weeks training, parade & gym, 3 weeks small arms, rifle and Bren-gun.
Gas training 14th week.
Nov. 13th, passed swimming, 4 lengths in duck test suit.
Nov. 24th, should have gone to gunnery.
Nov. 26th, transferred to Hayling for signalling, MNBDO (Mobile Naval Base Defence Organisation).
Dec. 18th, received Christmas parcel from Nell.'

Meanwhile Fort Cumberland and the training and development activities undertaken there, began to take a more war like appearance, with two pill boxes constructed and some of the gun emplacements modified to take anti-aircraft guns. Royal Marines manned 8 inch anti-aircraft guns from September 1939, under joint the joint Army and Naval Portsmouth Command. The two major units that had been using the fort up to

A Second World War searchlight or weapon support imposes itself in Fort Cumberland's North Bastion emplacement.

The barrel of a large coastal gun being installed by Royal Marines on Addu Atoll in the Pacific. This was accomplished as soon as it became apparent that Japan intended to enter the war. Some of the skills practiced by these men of the MNBDO can be seen in this photograph.

then had been the Inter Services Technical Development Centre (ISTDC), and the Mobile Naval Base Defence Nucleus that was soon to swap 'nucleus' for 'organisation' (MNBDO). Personnel were diverted from the former, whilst gunnery units from the latter were sent to build and man batteries at the naval anchorages in Scotland, and Alexandria in Egypt.

In September 1939 skeletal units were left at Fort Cumberland, for an air defence brigade headquarters, a signals company, fire control for 6 inch gun batteries and a Landing, Transport and Workshop (LTW) Company. The unit had a few tractors, six searchlights, training facilities for coastal defence artillery, including indirect fire control gear. It also had quantities of scaffolding and other materials for landing guns over beaches. The experience gained in the sixteen years to 1939 gave this organisation probably the most advanced techniques for the beach landing of heavy equipment of any service in the world. Having been situated alongside the ISTDC at Fort Cumberland, there was certainly unofficial liaison between these units.

Those remaining at Fort Cumberland joined MNBDO I on its formation. The war establishment of officers and five hundred and sixty-eight other ranks had been agreed by 17 May 1939, but the unit was not brought up to strength until 1940 as MNBDO I. In February 1940 A, B and 22 Light Batteries of Coast Defence Group had their headquarters in the fort.

The increase in 'HO' officers undertaking their training at the fort led to an additional officers' mess being opened.

Whilst Eastney Fort West had been left to become a solitary machine gun post, Eastney Fort East had been taken over by the Admiralty Signalling Establishment and had become a sea trials' station for radio location and power valve transmitters, along with aerial design. All sorts of assemblies for the radio location programme were made at ASE Eastney and many items, including aerials, were made by HM Dockyard, Portsmouth, using drawings produced at Eastney. Soon after the outbreak of war the Director of

Naval Ordnance asked whether a radar could be developed to provide accurate range on dive-bombers from 4,500m, down to about 900m. The 50cm waveband equipment was found to be capable and so it was moved to the anti-aircraft range at Eastney with antennae designed to be mounted on a pom-pom Mark II director so that they could be trained on the target visually. Trials took place in February 1940 and were sufficiently successful for the DNO representatives present to give unofficial approval to go ahead with the development. In April the official approval for the procurement of two hundred Type 282 sets was received from Admiralty. Antennae were redesigned for 30 MHz, and the first set was completed and installed at Eastney Fort East for trials in June 1940. Further radar development was undertaken in the fort both for the Admiralty and the War Office throughout the duration of the war, and after.

Some general types of direction finding ground radar were already in service and being combat tested as the 'Battle of Britain' began in earnest in the summer of 1940. Portsmouth Dockyard was always going to be a target for the Luftwaffe, but on the 26th August one of the many bombing raids on the city lost its bearings in poor visibility, which also hampered the intercepting Spitfires and Hurricanes. Around fifty Heinkel 111s of KG51 intending to bomb the submarine base at HMS *Dolphin*, Gosport, are thought to have turned north too soon, and on turning round to bomb on the return run, mistook the entrance to Langstone Harbour for the mouth of Portsmouth Harbour. As a result seventy eight bombs straddled Fort Cumberland, landing on the casements and bastions; one hit demolished a section killing eight officers and men.

This destroyed section of wall eventually became the new entrance to the fort as it was large enough to permit trucks inside the perimeter; a memorial plaque was mounted naming the men who died. The remaining damage was cleared and shored up, but remains unrepaired to this day. The MNBDO headquarters at the fort were closed on 4th February 1941, but the unit's specialist stores (ordnance) depot was established there by 1944. In 1945, the Technical Training Depot was running twenty trade courses, including drivers, mechanics and armourers. Four thousand Royal Marines trained at the fort during World War Two.

Eastney was not to escape unscarred from the air attack either; a stray bomb also landed in the open near the infirmary and the shock wave was powerful enough to break the plate glass windows in the Officers' Mess. As a result of this, and the bombing of Stonehouse Barracks in the Plymouth blitz where that mess suffered damage and loss, the three stained glass windows, representing Faith, Hope and Charity, at the top of the stairs in the mess were removed. Traditionally no Royal Marine officer ever descended the right-hand staircase, since this meant facing the Charity window, and no Royal Marine officer looks charity in the face. Some of the paintings and medals were also removed as a precaution, to be returned after May 1943

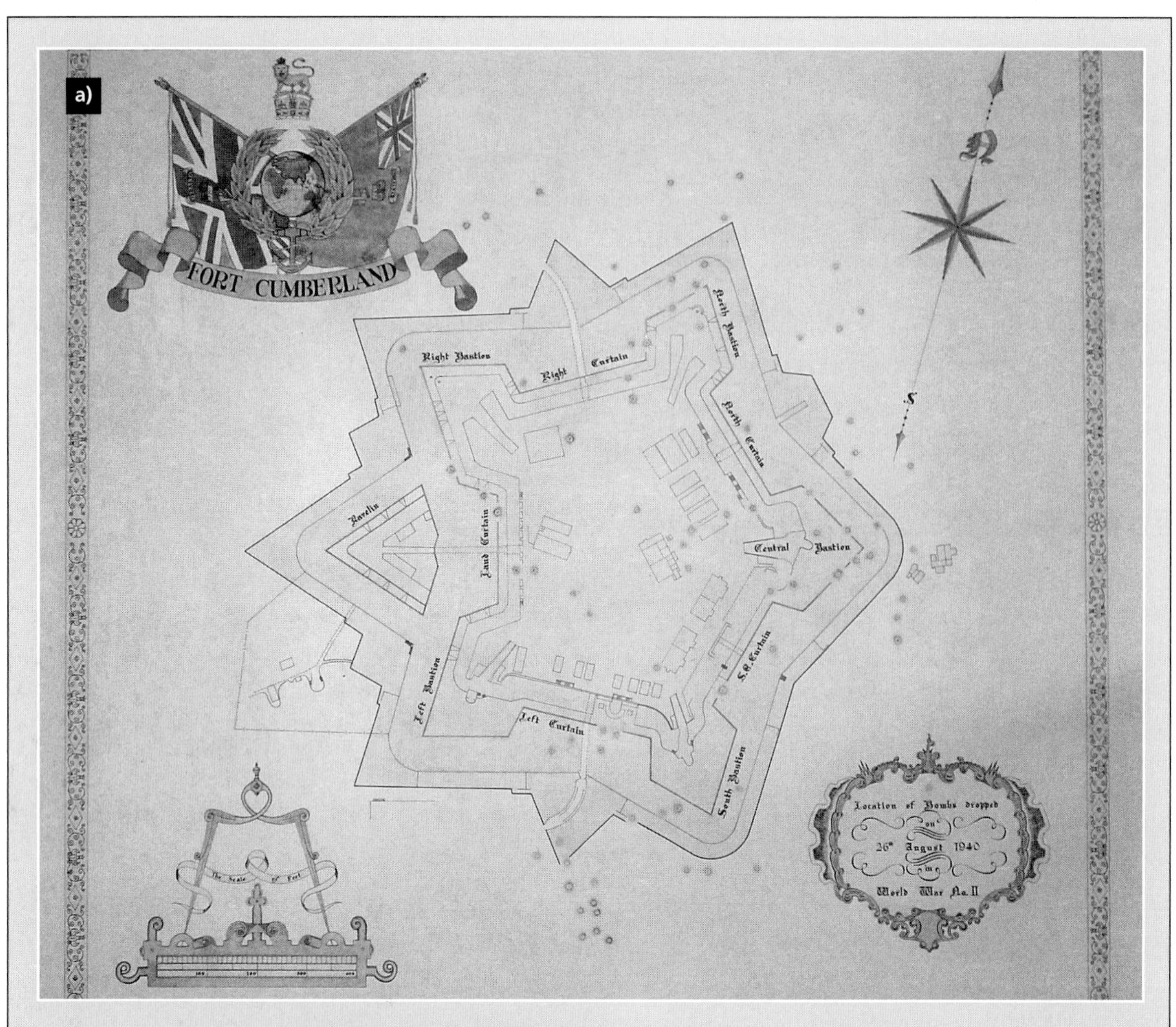

The Bombing of Fort Cumberland. a) This drawing shows the location of all the bombs that fell in the area of the fort during the raid of 26th August 1940. b) Bomb damage to some of the casements allows a glimpse of the internal construction of the fort. c) Buildings inside the fort were damaged by direct hits and by blast. d) The older, stronger, buildings were much more blast resistant. e) Bomb craters in the moat and damage to the walls themselves. Taken from the point of the Central Bastion looking towards the South Bastion. f) 2008 – Bomb damage to the walls of the South-East Curtain, close to the location of the now demolished tower seen in previous picture. g) 2008 – In the area of the Central Bastion huge concrete blocks positioned to support the bomb-damaged masonry resist the growth of natural vegetation. h) A recently installed memorial records the men of the Royal Marines who lost their lives during the attack. It has been placed on the central pillar of what became the fort's main entrance as a result of the heavy bomb damage to this part of the wall. The original plaque was moved to the Royal Marines Museum in 1973.

d)
e)
f)
g)
h)
IN MEMORY OF
THE OFFICERS AND MARINES
KILLED BY ENEMY ACTION
IN FORT CUMBERLAND
ON 26TH AUG. 1940. DURING
THE BATTLE OF BRITAIN.
TEMP. 2ND LT. C. B. HOBHOUSE.
" " " H.G. JAMESON.
" " " E. A. P. HILLAND.
" " " A.T. C. HOCKING.
" " " P. W. FITZJOHN.
MARINE HAROLD WATSON.
" D. J. HOPKINS.
" B. J. COOKE.

when it was deemed the threat had passed. The replacement plain glass windows however made the hall lighter and it was decided not to reinstall the originals after the war.

Having been defeated in the Battle of Britain, the Luftwaffe tried to maintain an air offensive throughout 1941 and 1942 with tactical night bombing and also through daylight harassing raids with improved marks of their fighters converted into fighter-bombers. Often operating in pairs the Messerchmitts, and the new Focke-Wulf 190s, would fly in from France fast and low to avoid detection, and strafe and bomb targets of opportunity before escaping interception. One such attack fell on Eastney witnessed by Marine Alfred Hewitt:-

'In the Summer of 1942, two squads of Royal Marines, 167 HO of which I was a member, and the 176 Regulars, were rehearsing ceremonial drills on the parade ground furthest from the Officers Mess at about 2.30 pm.

'Suddenly a German plane appeared from behind the Officers' Mess and strafed the parade ground. Some 176 squad members were wounded and fell to the ground and Sergeant Howard in charge of my squad, ordered me to take over as he was going to help with the wounded.

The plane which had strafed us was returning to join a second German plane which was circling behind the Officers' Mess at a height of approximately 800 feet.

'I immediately ordered 167 Squad to "Open Order March" as I considered that we must present the smallest possible target by attaining more

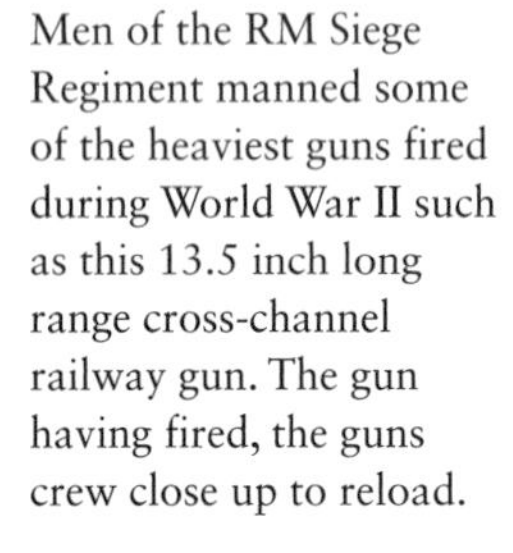

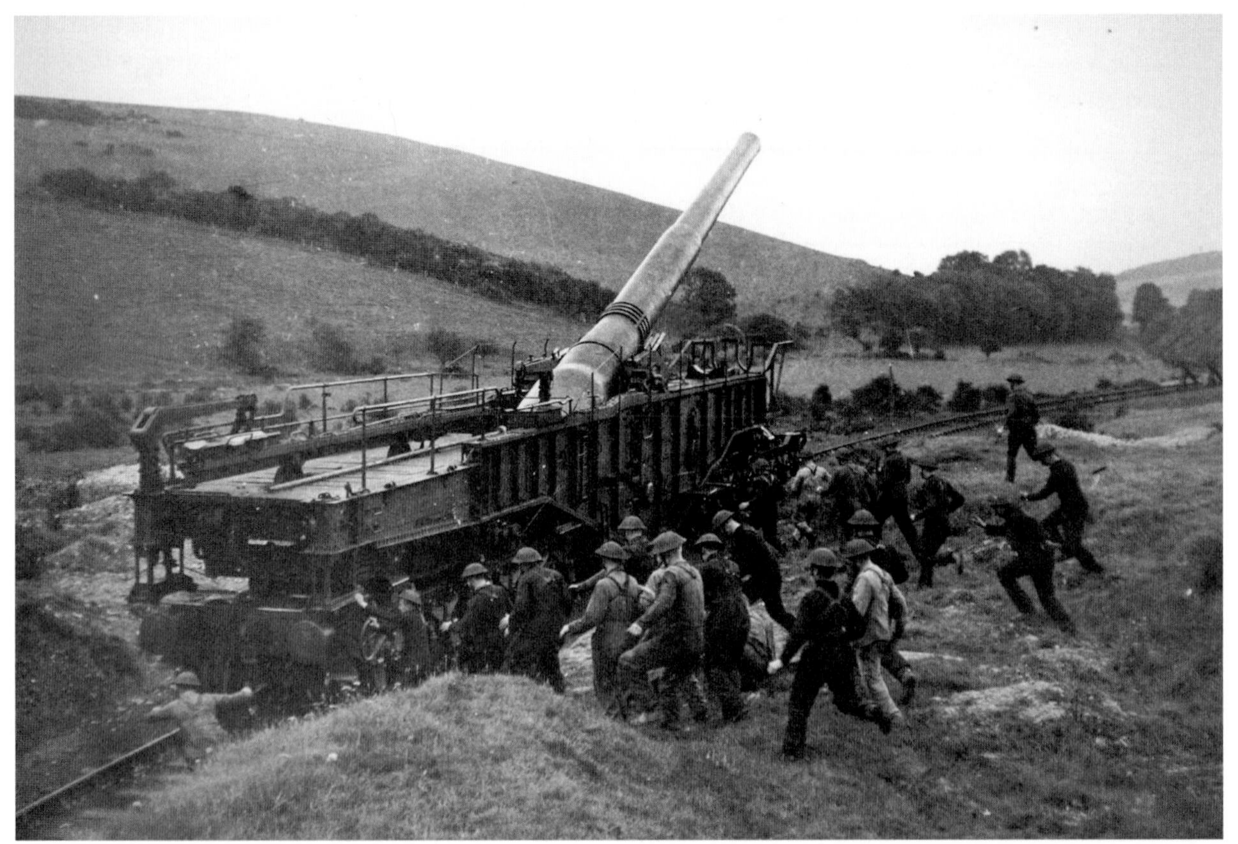

Men of the RM Siege Regiment manned some of the heaviest guns fired during World War II such as this 13.5 inch long range cross-channel railway gun. The gun having fired, the guns crew close up to reload.

'Bruce' a long range gun at St Margaret's Bay, Kent, in 1943.

space between ranks. By this time 176 Squad had succeeded in carrying their wounded clear of the parade ground into the drill shed by the eastern access.'

The plane strafed the squad and passed over Alfred Hewitt's head and ceased fire. 'I had not been hit, nor had any member of 167 Squad. I gave the orders "Right Turn" and "To the Drill Shed Quick March". We were entering the drill shed by the western access and almost clear of the parade ground when the second German plane flew past and fired a prolonged burst of machine gun fire. About 50-60 bullets zipped past my right arm and slurped along the ground midway between two files of marines facing me and as far as the second rank. Fortunately, no-one was hit. I ordered 167 Squad to lie down in the drill shed a few yards east of the drill shed clock. Almost immediately there was a loud explosion from just outside the barracks. We all felt the effect of the blast; the clock face shattered with glass flying in all directions and when I looked up it had stopped at 2.50 pm.'

Commended for his action, Alfred was granted a commission and promoted to temporary Lieutenant on 24th January 1943. He went on to serve in the Far East with RM Detachment 385, a forerunner of the SBS.

An earlier Royal Marine unit with connections to the SBS was also training and operating at Eastney and Lumps Fort. In 1942 the Royal Marines Boom Patrol Detachment were training for a canoe raid to mine German blockade runners using the port of Bordeaux up the Gironde River. With their headquarters in Dolphin Court, opposite Canoe Lake in Southsea, the unit name was a cover to enable them to be seen canoeing in the Solent, ostensibly inspecting the anti submarine boom that had been built

Gunnery training continued throughout the Second World War.

The 1st Heavy Anti-Aircraft Regiment, Royal Marines, was deployed in defence against flying bomb attacks on south-east England. A 3.7 inch gun's crew are loading their gun which is located at Dunes Farm near Tunbridge Wells, Kent

to protect the naval base. The twelve man team would launch their attack from the HM Submarine *Tuna* at the mouth of the river, then paddle up to the ships anchored in the port, attach delayed action limpet mines and make good their escape. The raid, codenamed 'Operation Frankton' took place on the night of 7th December 1942, and resulted in five ships being damaged. Unfortunately only Major 'Blondie' Hasler and his canoe partner Marine Bill Sparkes, survived to escape via Spain and Gibraltar to return to England.

Following the success of Op Frankton, the raid on shipping in Bordeaux Harbour, the development and use of the canoe continued in the waters of Eastney and also in its swimming pool. Experimental craft, like this catamaran canoe created by joining two two-man canoes, were tried, some successfully – others not so. A note on the back of this photograph says: 'MC had another canoe like this with oil driven outboard – so loud it was worthless'. This photograph was probably taken off Hayling Island.

'Pilot' training in a 'Sleeping Beauty' or Motorised Submersible Canoe (MSC) in Eastney swimming pool c1945. Lesson eight in the syllabus required the 'pilot' to wear the rubber UWSS (underwater swim suit) with the self contained underwater breathing apparatus, otherwise known as SCUBA.

In spite of the losses to the unit, its experimental work and use and development of canoes continued, and for one project the barracks swimming pool was called into use. Hasler had seen the value of attacking ships from beneath the water after Italian frogmen had successfully damaged HMS *Valiant* and HMS *Queen Elizabeth* in Alexandria Harbour in December 1941. A submersible canoe that could be paddled or sailed on the surface, then piloted as a type of mini submarine, using a small motor, propeller and hydroplanes, near to the target was developed. Nick-named the 'Sleeping Beauty' the Motorised Submersible Canoe (MSC) was first produced by Camper & Nicholson in Gosport, and underwent trials in Staines Reservoir and Eastney pool, in the summer of 1943. Hasler, as the canoeist, experimented with the use of the Davis Submarine Escape Apparatus when the vessel was submerged. This pioneered the development of the Self Contained Underwater Breathing Apparatus, or SCUBA as is now known.

Major Hasler later went on to command Detachment 385, based in Ceylon (Sri Lanka).

For the most part Eastney Barracks specialised in sea service gunnery and training ships detachments for service afloat; much as it had done for the RMA in the First World War. The sea service batteries acquired further types of guns as the war progressed, but it was not lost on the instructors that most of later types were pointing ever skyward. The big gun Navy was in decline; the new threat was from the air, and even as the Royal Marines accepted this, the move within the Corps was to the Commando role – a role that would ultimately save the Royal Marines from possible disbandment.

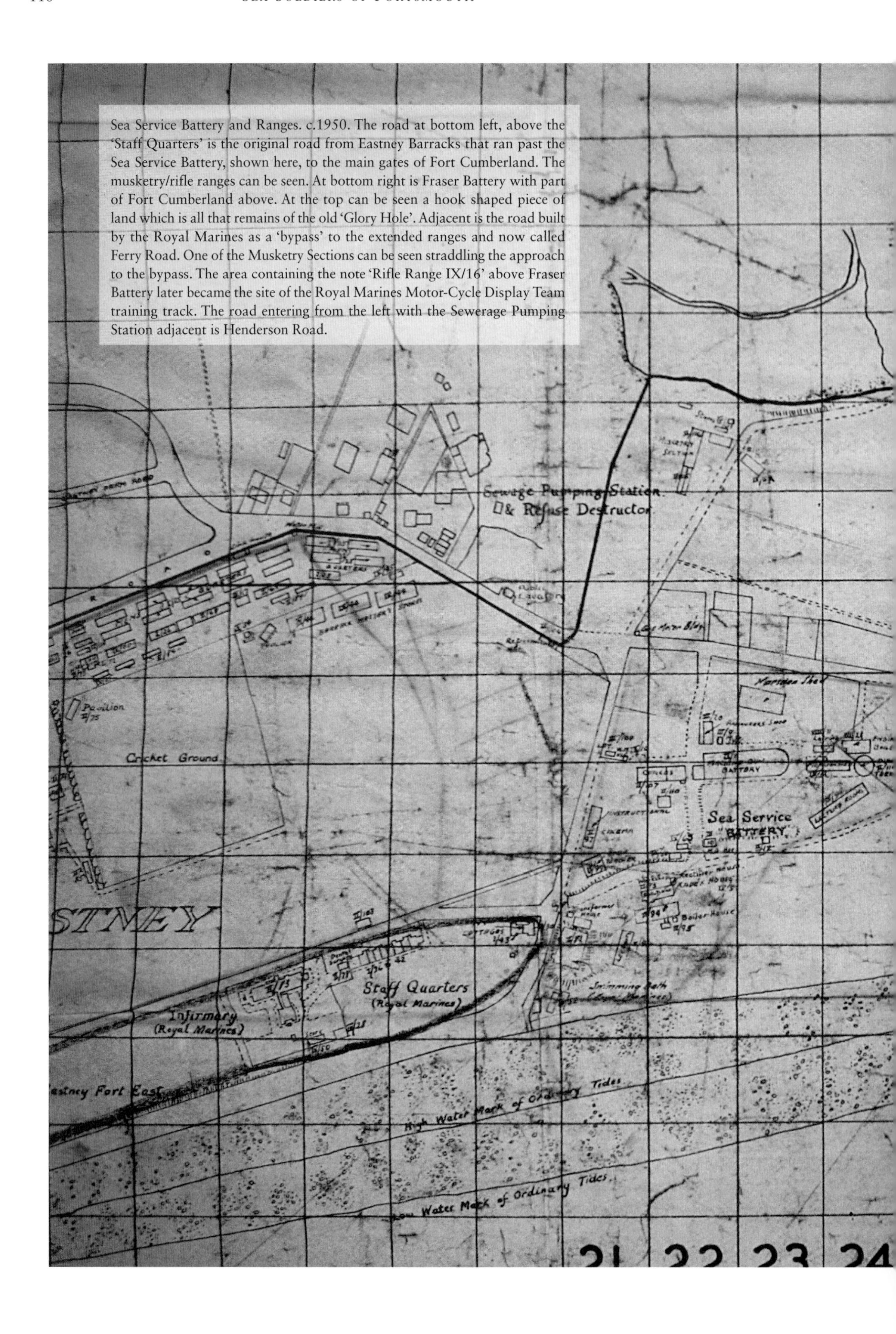

Sea Service Battery and Ranges. c.1950. The road at bottom left, above the 'Staff Quarters' is the original road from Eastney Barracks that ran past the Sea Service Battery, shown here, to the main gates of Fort Cumberland. The musketry/rifle ranges can be seen. At bottom right is Fraser Battery with part of Fort Cumberland above. At the top can be seen a hook shaped piece of land which is all that remains of the old 'Glory Hole'. Adjacent is the road built by the Royal Marines as a 'bypass' to the extended ranges and now called Ferry Road. One of the Musketry Sections can be seen straddling the approach to the bypass. The area containing the note 'Rifle Range IX/16' above Fraser Battery later became the site of the Royal Marines Motor-Cycle Display Team training track. The road entering from the left with the Sewerage Pumping Station adjacent is Henderson Road.

Mud
Fort Cumberland
Ryle Range
Fort
Cumberland
Targets
Targets
31 32 33 34
26 27 28 29 30

10 **Post War Eastney**

AFTER THE demobilisation of the Second World War, the inevitable reduction of man-power stimulated a reorganisation the Royal Marines and their future role. Having just endured a global war, the political and military thought was restricted to considering and defending against a future one of atomic and nuclear capability. For the Navy, the aircraft carrier eclipsed the battleship, and the missile eclipsed the gun. This was to affect the Royal Marines' traditional role in serving at sea.

Presentation of Colours at Eastney in 1956. The wartime blast shelters are still visible in front of the main barrack block.

An unusual view that shows the proximity of the various sites. The tree line in the background is Haying Island, with the buildings of the centre of Fort Cumberland in front, Fraser Battery on the far right and the Marsden Shed of the sea service school on the far left. The roofs of the staff sergeant's quarters can be seen on the right with the Officers' Mess block at Eastney in the foreground.

A Gunnery Instructor explains the operation of a breach in the Instructional Turret to a group of recruits c.1952. This is one of the two guns, by now upgraded to 15 inch, in the gun turret.

A post- Second World War 4.5 inch gun in N Battery at the Gunnery School, Royal Marines.

By 1947 gunnery and naval training for the Corps was centralized in the Gunnery School and Eastney Barracks. Naval training consisted of seamanship, damage control, ship fire-fighting and naval gunnery. The school functioned as a unit, with its own Commandant, Staff Officers and Gunnery Instructors, and was divided into a long-range section, and another for close-range instruction, which included anti-aircraft guns.

The real thing. Royal Marines man their 40mm Bofors anti-aircraft gun on board an aircraft-carrier c.1952.

In 1949 a modernisation of the Sea Service Battery removed the 6-inch Mark XII guns, which were replaced by two triple 6-inch Mark XXIII mock-up turrets. Nearby the 'Battle Teacher' (a simulator for gunnery training) was fitted with modern sound effects, which were extremely loud. At this time, around two thousand of all ranks were passing through training in the school each year. In 1951 a rolling platform carrying two power-operated turrets with gyro gun-sights, better films and sound effects and an electronic hit recorder, was added.

However, by 1956 there were only some twenty detachments in major warships and a dozen in smaller ships, totalling only two thousand Royal Marines at sea.

The naval gun changed from an offensive armament to a defensive one – to protect the ship; firstly from aircraft, eventually from missiles. As the calibre reduced, the rate of fire increased, the range got shorter, the speed of aim had to get quicker. Soon it was not expected to hit a jet with a shell or bullet – the gunnery navy was a thing of the past.

The Crinoline Church Bell that after 1906, was used as the ship's bell for the Sea Service Gunnery School

On 30 June 1958 the Gunnery School closed down and gunnery training transferred to HMS *Excellent*. By October the last six heavy guns were removed and work started on the dismantling of the Instructional Turret. The ship's bell in the school was salvaged as it had originally been hung in the old 'Crinoline' Church, at the barracks until 1906.

It was perhaps an indicator of the new direction the Corps would take, when two of the last Instructor Officers, Lieutenant Brown and Captain Stanley Kemp both went on to serve in the newly converted Commando Carrier, HMS *Bulwark*.

Meanwhile a fundamental change had already occurred for the Royal Marines, when in 1947 the traditional 'Divisions' had been restructured as

The Rundown of the Sea Service Battery a) The western end of the Royal Marines Gunnery School c.1955. The large building on the left was the 'Battle Teacher' whilst the long, low, building consisted of instructional rooms and a cinema. Behind this building is Henderson Road and the Nissen huts of Melville Camp. b) This continuation image shows the offices of Pay and Records Office, Royal Marines in what was once the Machine Gun Shed and the small parade in front. The Crinoline Church bell, now in the Museum, can be seen hanging from a wooden stand close to the flagpole. The building to the right is the end of the Sea Service Battery. Beyond the offices can be seen the old Musketry Section buildings. c) The whole of the Sea Service Battery, by now rarely used for gunnery instruction, can be seen in this view. Behind it is the Marsden Shed and the view across Eastney Lake towards the St James area. The gates in the foreground are on Old Ferry Road. d) This view of the eastern end of the Royal Marines Gunnery School shows the end of the Sea Service battery with, alongside it, the Machine Gun Shed and then the Instructional Turret. In front of these are the Lecture Room building and various turrets and guns. Beyond the Lecture Room building is the hump marking the location of Proe's Pond, by now the site of a sewerage tank. Beyond this can be seen the ramparts of Fort Cumberland, the boat shed in the ravelin and other buildings within the Fort. The area between these two major locations contains the ranges.

Fort Cumberland with Fraser Battery at the top right of the picture. Between the ravelin and Fraser Battery is the site of the High Angle Mortar Battery. Wooden sheds appear to have been erected in the emplacements.

'groups' with Eastney now being the headquarters of Portsmouth Group, RM. This modernisation incorporated the move to the Corps being a Commando equipped amphibious force. It also spelt the end of Chatham Barracks that closed in 1950, and was demolished about five years later. As a result, the Pay and Records Office, Royal Marines (PRORM) transferred from Melville Barracks, along with the name, to Eastney, and lodged themselves into the wartime hutment camp, which became Melville Camp. They would later gain 'Drafting' to their title and move to the converted 'gun-less' sea service battery buildings. The record office element of this organisation would be a supporting factor when the Royal Marines Museum was established in the old school building near the barracks' main gate in 1958.

Another transfer from Chatham of a different scale had been Marine H W Nicholls and his pigeons in October 1947, prior to the moving of the Chatham Signal School. A pigeon loft was built into the recruit block at Eastney that he had served in nine years before when he joined the Royal

'Curious Curates'. A group of young officers at Eastney, dressed as Parsons, pose for their photograph before a 'run ashore' to see a famous stripper at a local variety theatre. c.1954.

Marines in 283 Squad in April 1938 (he had later transferred to Chatham). Upon arrival he collected a further twenty pigeons shipped from the USA at Portsmouth Airport, and on one occasion was asked to follow the Commandant by car with a basket full, to release them from Winchester Station to see how long they took to travel back to Eastney.

In 1954 Warwick Films began filming 'The Cockleshell Heroes' based on the 'Operation Frankton' raid conducted by RMBPD on German shipping in Bordeaux in December 1942. The Commandant General was keen to highlight a Royal-Marines-based major film production, and allowed the company access and assistance from the Corps. Much of the initial footage was shot at Eastney Barracks, Fort Cumberland, Fraser Battery and Southsea, while the river Tagus in Portugal substituted for the Gironde in France. The title march 'Cockleshell Heroes' was especially written and performed by Lt Col F Vivian Dunn and the RM Band. Colonel 'Blondie' Hasler and Corporal Bill Sparkes, the survivors from the actual raid, were initially employed as technical advisors. Hasler was to later distance himself from the film. Royal Marines from the City of London RMFVR and a detachment under Captain R M Brounger RM assisted and trained the actors, with Corporals Richens and Close, saving Trevor Howard and David Lodge from drowning on one occasion when they capsized. When released in 1955, it was the first British film to be shot in Cinemascope, and provided early minor roles for Anthony Newley and Sam Kydd. Within the film's production team was Albert Broccoli, later to direct many James Bond Films.

Shortly after the end of the Second World War Lord Fraser inspected the Technical Training Wing in Fort Cumberland. This is believed to be the only occasion when the TTW paraded with the Portsmouth Colour.

At Fort Cumberland the Technical Training Wing and the Amphibious School co-habited during the late 1940s and early 1950s. The Amphibious School absorbed many of the wartime raiding and amphibious units to

Above: Captains Roberts and Stewart of the Royal Marine Boom Patrol Detachment wearing Under Water Swimmers Suit Mk 1 with Types A & B hoods and American fins. To the right is Major 'Blondie' Hasler. The date is 28th May 1943, approximately two months after 'Blondie' reached the United Kingdom following his escape through France and Spain having led the successful Op Frankton raid.

Above centre: Men of the SBS practice from a Landing Craft, Assault, in Langstone Harbour 1948.

Above right: Frogman from the Amphibious School Royal Marines, at Fort Cumberland, training in Langstone harbour.

Right: Canoeists of the Special Boat Section.

Frogman parachuting into the Solent.

provide a centre for training and development. In 1949 it took in the Combined Operations Beach and Boat Section (COBBS) which had already absorbed wartime units specializing in frogmen, canoe raids, airborne operations, demolition raiding and reconnaissance intelligence behind enemy lines. The wing continued to develop its clandestine work, and by 1951 it had been renamed the Special Boat Wing. Swimmer-canoeists were trained in techniques of small-scale reconnaissance and raiding, with a variety of dories, inflatables, canoes, surf boats, swimmer-delivery units (SDUs) and paddle boards. The first parachute descent into water took place in the Solent in April 1951, adding parachuting to the training. No. 1 Special Boat Section was stationed at the Amphibious School at this time. Alongside the Special Boat Wing, the school had the Landing Craft Wing and Beach Wing. Crews were trained for the three main types of minor landing craft: the LCA (assault), LCM (mechanized) and LCP (personnel). Other amphibious equipment and experimental craft were also evaluated. To maintain the craft and other equipment there was a detachment of Royal Navy officers and ratings.

The Beach Wing consisted of the Royal Naval Beach Control Party (RNBCP), Landing Craft Obstacle Clearance Unit (LCOCU) and the Landing Craft Recovery Unit (LCRU). These units had evolved and developed their techniques from the experience of amphibious landings during the Second World War and they were to develop their capabilities and methods with the new equipment that was being trialled.

In 1951 the first amphibious 'Exercise Runaground' in the Solent and on Eastney beach was undertaken. For the Royal Marines it demonstrated how the new group organisation was to work with Portsmouth Group responsible for sea service and amphibious training, and Plymouth Group responsible for military and Commando training. The exercise would demonstrate a possible sequence of events in an amphibious assault on a defended coast, and involved warships, landing craft, tanks, infantry, the SBS, and mock air strikes. Helicopters and Hovercraft made their public debuts at these proceedings, even though they were principally run for the benefit of the Defence Staff and visiting guests every year. The exception was 1956, when the Suez crisis involved doing one for real at Port Said.

In 1954 the Amphibious School moved out of Fort Cumberland to HMS *Turtle* the old Landing Craft base at Poole.

The Technical Training Wing was a post war version of the depot that had functioned in the fort during World War Two. Many of the skills of the MNBDO group were still being developed and in early 1945 the depot ran courses for twenty trades including drivers, surveyors, and gun fitters. By 1958 it was organised into three sections; driver and motor cyclist platoon, technical trades, and group workshops. Trades undertaken were:

- Armourer (small arms)
- Bricklayer/Plumber
- Carpenter
- Coach trimmer
- Draughtsman (mechanical and topographical)
- Electrician (vehicle and plant)
- Painter
- Printer
- Sheet Metal worker/welder
- Storeman/clerk (technical)
- Vehicle Mechanic/Armament Artificer

The training in these skills enabled Royal Marines to be self-sufficient within its units, and the work continued after the wing transferred to Poole in 1973.

Further development took place in the area between the Officers' Mess and Fort Cumberland as the Admiralty took over land for naval married quarters. Between 1955 and 1956, three estates were created. The Esplanade Gardens estate was constructed on the allotments between Eastney Fort East

The crest of the Small Raids Wing that was hung at Fort Cumberland. It was drawn and painted by Mne Boarman who was later invalided from the Corps as the result of injuries sustained in an explosion. The crest shows a Frog, representing the underwater swimming part of reconnaissance or raids on shipping. Parachute Wings represent an approach to a target by air. Crossed Paddles represent a surface approach to a target ashore, or afloat, by canoe or inflatable boat from a fast coastal vessel or submarine. All ranks of the SRW received training in all three methods of approach during a two-year tour in the wing. Prior to 1949, Small Operations Group South East Asia Command was reduced to a cadre known as the School of Combined Operations Beach and Boat Section which, in 1948, was amalgamated with the Royal Marines Boom Patrol Detachment to form the Small Raids Wing of the Amphibious School, Royal Marines whose HQ was in Fort Cumberland.

Ex- Runaground was carried out by units of the Royal Marines over a number of years during the 1950s at Eastney. a) reconnaissance of the beach is carried out, then b) a path is cleared of mines to allow c) the RN Beach Party to set-up their advanced post – in the background the buildings of Fraser Battery and the Gunnery School. d) The landing craft run in towards the beach and e) men start coming ashore (note the sea fort in the background).

2008. Looking northwards along Eastney Point to the narrow neck between Eastney and Hayling Island. The gorse and scrub covered land and the foreshore on the left bears little testament to the trials and training, the experiments and exercises that took place here over a period of almost a hundred years.

and the infirmary. At the same time a development of fifty houses for other ranks and ratings was built on the land north of the Gunnery School (Fort Cumberland Road), with three shops added later. The third estate was built beyond Melville Camp and the rugby pitch, comprising of six blocks containing a total of forty-eight flats, and five houses. This was named Halliday Crescent after Captain Lewis Halliday, who won the Victoria Cross in 1900, at the siege of Peking. After the demolition of the infirmary buildings, the Crescent became connected to the housing built on the site at Driftwood Gardens.

On the 14th May 1959, The Royal Marines received the freedom of the City of Portsmouth. The Captain-General, Prince Phillip, arrived at Eastney

The former naval quarters of Finch and Gibraltar Roads were built on the infill of the 'Glory Hole'at Eastney Lake, as well as the sites of the musketry huts and ranges. The foreground of this photograph is the site of the RM Motor Cycle Display Team track.

Technical Trades The wide range of trades taught at Fort Cumberland allowed the Royal Marines to be virtually self-supporting. a) Driver, b) radio operator, c) bricklayer student screeding, d) signwriter, e) sheet metal worker, f) draughtsman, g) a forge in one of the casements, h) carpenter/joiner, i) printer, j) vehicle mechanic, k) welder.

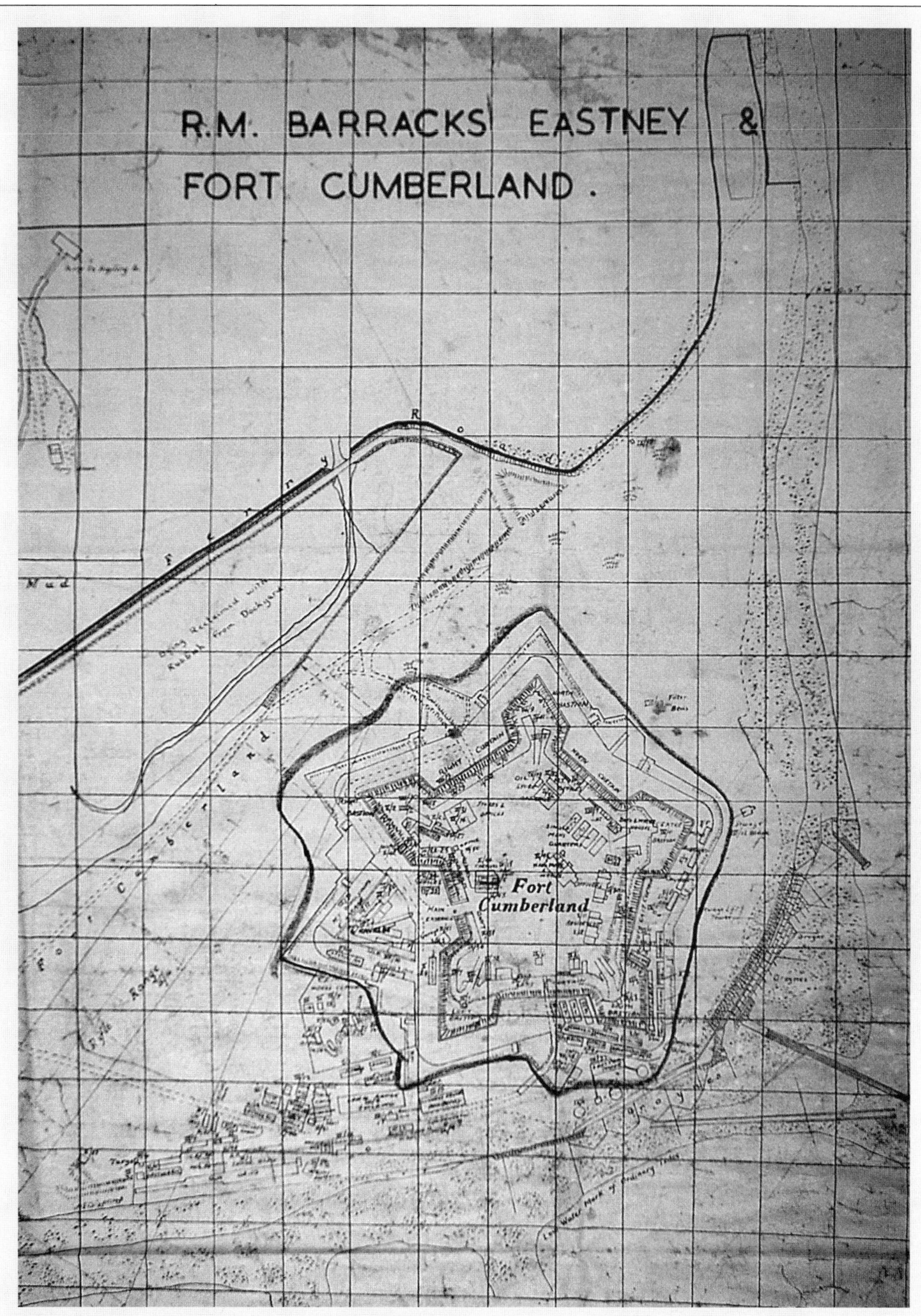

Fort Cumberland c.1950. A previous owner of this drawing has outlined Fort Cumberland with a wax pencil. The shape and the evidence of the long-term occupation and building can be seen although, even on the original, some of the annotation is difficult to read. The relationship of the fort to the Southsea shoreline, the Langstone Harbour Channel and Eastney Lake can be clearly seen. The coffin-shape below the '&' in the drawing title is the site of the old Point Battery The inset to the left is an extension to the main plan and shows the point and the Hayling Island ferry building and jetty.

Aerial view of Eastney from the east shows the hutted camp to the right of centre and also development around the edge of the sports fields. The Junior Officers' Accomodation hut can be seen close to the shore where the entrance to the museum now is, and the remains of the old Gunnery School are in the bottom left corner.

at ten o'clock and inspected three companies with the Colours of 42 and 45 Commandos, the Royal Marines Association, and the RM Old Comrades Association whose ranks included General Lewis Halliday VC, and Lieutenant Norman Finch VC. Fittingly it was Halliday's birthday that day; he was 89. A fanfare especially composed by Lt Col Vivian Dunn was sounded and the freedom scroll was read by the Town Clerk, Mr V Blanchard. Before the Royal Marines exercised their new right to march through the city to the Guildhall, the Captain General made his first visit to the RM Museum that had formed the year before. He was to return in August 1975 to re-open it in the former Officers' Mess, and has visited on a number of other occasions in its development since then.

The Royal Marines Exhibition of September 1958. The layout of Eastney Fort West can also be seen in this view.

Within the barracks, new building and conversions also took place beginning with Teapot Row when it was converted into flats in 1955. The centre pillar of the main gate was removed in 1967 to enable trucks and coaches easier access.

There followed a three phase development of Eastney in the

HRH Prince Philip, Captain General Royal Marines, receives the Freedom Casket from the Lord Mayor of Portsmouth at Eastney Barracks, 14th July 1959. Both the casket and the scroll are in the Royal Marines Museum Collections. The Lord Mayor was Alfred Blake, a former Royal Marine officer.

The Freedom of the City of Portsmouth Ceremony – the march to the Guildhall.

Eastney Fort West and the officers' accommodation (Teapot Row) from seaward during the 1950s.

The main gate of Eastney Barracks in Cromwell Road c1908. The centre pillar was removed for better vehicle access in 1967.

1960s. The first phase included the accommodation of Wrens at the barracks, with officers quarters being converted for female use and a substantial block of flats being built on the old Sergeants' Mess tennis courts. These quarters provided accommodation for Wrens serving in Portsmouth Naval Base as well as the 'Marens' detachment at Eastney. Work commenced in August 1964 and was completed at the beginning of 1966. By 1970 the detachment consisted of three officers, eleven Senior Ratings and one hundred and fifteen Junior Ratings. The 'Marens' detachment provided clerical staff for the offices and departments of the barracks, including the Headquarters Portsmouth Group, the Corps Instructor Officer, the *Globe & Laurel,* and DPRORM.

The second phase was the building of the new Sergeants' Mess between the playing fields and St Andrew's Church, which was opened in 1967. Upon completion, the former mess on the northern side of the Drill Shed became the junior NCOs club. After the 1973 reduction of the barracks, the accommodation was taken over by the Headquarters Training Group for use by all ranks.

The final phase was to be the rebuilding of Melville Camp for the Signals and Technical Training Wing, but defence cuts and the withdrawal from

This image, recently taken from the ramparts of Eastney Fort East, shows the relationship between some of the components of the RMA facility. Between the houses can be seen the swimming pool (partly obscured by a single tree); the caravan park which is opposite the site of the Sea Service Battery; and the buildings and antennae of Fraser Battery. The two shed-like buildings stand within the ravelin of Fort Cumberland.

A number of Searchlight Tattoos were held on the Main Parade during the 1980's. They were produced by the Royal Marines Museum Director, Colonel Keith Wilkins OBE, with a great deal of support from the Corps. The 1988 Tattoo was the largest of its kind to be staged in the South of England and was a major joint-Service event. Not only were two Royal Marine Bands on parade but so were massed bands of the British Army. Here we see, in the dusk of a late summers evening the Massed Bands of the Royal Electrical and Mechanical Engineers, the St Georges Band of the Royal Regiment of Fusiliers and the Corps of Drums of the 2nd Battalion Scots Guards, marching onto the Main Parade.

Aden altered the plans.

In January 1968, Eastney became the headquarters for a RM Commando unit for the first and only time, as 43 Commando made the move from Plymouth to make space for 45 Commando returning from Aden. They were destined for a Second World War experience in Melville Camp had it not been for a combination of staff from Drafting, Pay and Records Office and an advance party from 43 Commando modernising the huts. The withdrawal of 45 Commando from Aden had been brought forward, as the unit correspondent at Plymouth wrote in the *Globe & Laurel:-*

'At this stage we welcomed the first of 45 Commando's advance party to the Barracks. Their task was simplified thanks to the plan for the move. A much depleted 43 Commando was to move to Portsmouth, the remainder of the Unit was to remain in Plymouth and become 45 Commando, thus giving the incoming unit some men who already knew the ropes. For many it will mean just changing their lanyards at the appropriate moment — from old gold and scarlet to red at Stonehouse and vice versa for "repats" from Aden who go straight to Eastney to join us.'

After reforming in 1961 at Plymouth, 43 Commando had become the public relations Commando with a busy schedule of public engagements, tournaments, shows, demonstrations and even fêtes when not on exercises. They had been tasked with recruitment at a time when the Campaign for Nuclear Disarmament, the hippy movement and anti-Vietnam war sentiments had spread to Britain from the USA, and not for the first or last time, the armed services were losing popularity with the youth of the country. On the one hand the Royal Marines fostered acceptance from 'pop' culture and the 'swinging sixties' with the Radio 1 DJ Jimmy Saville becoming a life-long supporter of the Corps'; making numerous public and charity appearances with the Royal Marines. On the other hand the short haired serviceman was struggling with his off-duty image to the extent that the *Globe & Laurel* ran adverts at this time for 'the weekender wig' that would hide the short back and sides of the hapless, 'square', marine on leave.

On 20th February Melville Camp was officially renamed Comacchio Camp by General Sir Norman Tailyour and Lady Tailyour. 'Comacchio Hall' had also been built, and as reported in the unit news sheet – 'the Mess Committee is going ahead with the purchase of amenities. A colour TV has been rented, and an ice-making machine purchased for the bar; a coffee-making machine has been obtained, on unusual but advantageous terms. Hot coffee can be produced in four minutes, but the caterer, John Boffin, on his initial test run, took one and a half hours, and finished up with water spurting from every joint, nook and cranny'.

1968 being a leap year, the 43 Commando unit diary entry read 'all unmarried ranks in hiding' against the date February 29th! On Saturday 18th May it recorded 'the FA Cup final shown on colour TV in the NAAFI to a good crowd. The bar was open all afternoon'. The final between West Bromwich Albion and Everton was the first final televised live in colour. Albion won by a single goal.

Unfortunately, about this time, the decision was made to disband 43 Commando and personnel were dispersed to the remaining Commando units on 1st October. Just before that, on the 5th September, Sgt J R Newman, fishing off Eastney, caught a 31lb 10oz sea trout, which was later ratified as a national record.

A farewell parade was scheduled for the 26th September, and two days before, the unit officers were invited for drinks at the Senior NCOs Mess. Of a less formal nature Colour Sergeant Waldron had organised a Stag Night at the RMA club consisting of 'two strippers, two comedians and a large amount of beer at 6d a pint – it was a successful evening'.

In 1969 Eastney was designated Training Group Royal Marines, and the following year a report listed the complement as:-

- A Headquarters Company
- A Band and Drums Company
- A General Training Company
- An Independent Commando Company (R Company)
- Signal Training Wing, Royal Marines (including Clerks Training)
- Technical Training Wing, Royal. Marines
- A WRNS detachment
- The equivalent of a company of civilians
- The Corps Inspectorate of Physical Training
- The Corps Museum and Archives
- The Offices of the *Globe and Laurel* Magazine
- The Central Office of the Royal Marines Association
- The Portsmouth Detachment of Royal Marines Reserve, City of London

It provided services for:

(a) Headquarters, Portsmouth Group, Royal Marines

(b) Drafting, Pay and Records Office, Royal Marines (DPRORM)

(c) Falkland Islands Detachment
(d) Most ranks on detached duties in the UK

The divisional school building that originally stood to the left of the main barracks' gate in Cromwell Road. Partially converted to married quarters in 1904, the building eventually became the RM Museum in 1958. It was demolished in 1984.

In 1971 it was announced that there would be a major reduction to Eastney. The Technical and Signals Training Wings would leave, and only the Headquarters Training Group, Corps Museum, the *Globe and Laurel*, Royal Marines Association and the Royal Marines Band would remain. The computerisation of service records began the following year, which required DPRORM to move to a larger site and to combine with the Royal Navy's personnel records. They eventually located at HMS *Centurion* at Gosport.

The Wrens block, latterly the Band block, being demolished. The Royal Marine Association building is in the centre. The Sergeants' Mess has been demolished.

By 1973 the 'contraction' of Eastney had taken place, and although the Royal Marines Training Reserve Forces headquarters had reorganised and remained, the barracks was emptying and running down. After launching an appeal, the Royal Marines Museum relocated to the centre section of the Officers Mess, and was re-opened on 1st August 1975.

In April 1983 the Recruit Blocks, the old School, Signals School and NAAFI were demolished to make way for one hundred and seventeen houses

View from the site of Proe's Pond , which became a sewage tank, looking east along Fort Cumberland Road 2008.

together with roads, footpaths and car parking facilities on land accessed off Henderson Road. This development by Wimpey Homes became what is known as Lidiard Gardens.

'Comacchio Camp' had been pulled down in 1976, and in June 1983 planning permission was granted for the construction of forty-nine two-storey houses with garage facilities, again accessed off Henderson Road. Work commenced on this site in November 1983, and this became Cockleshell Gardens, named after the popular name for the 'Operation Frankton' raid. On the 27th March 1987 the MP for Portsmouth South, Mike Hancock, raised questions in the Commons about the future of Eastney Barracks including what organisations were still present. In reply the Secretary of State for Defence listed the following:

1. Headquarters Training Reserve and Special Forces Royal Marines;
2. A small secretariat responsible for administration of non-public funds within the Royal Marines;
3. The editor of the Royal Marines magazine, "Globe and Laurel", and his staff;
4. The Royal Marines Museum;
5. The Royal Marines' Historical Archivist;
6. A small Royal Marines Reserve detachment;
7. A detachment of the Royal Marine Volunteer Cadet Corps;
8. An official of the Property Services Agency also has an office in the barracks.

He also added 'It is the intention to proceed as quickly as possible with the disposal of the Eastney Barracks site once the extent of any residual Royal Marines' presence there has been determined. The future of the Eastney playing fields will depend upon the outcome of a separate study'.

The weather also played its part in the reduction of Eastney when the storms of October 1987 displaced many slates from the roofs of the buildings and brought down some of the older trees bordering the Main Parade. The winds were strong enough in one gust to bend the hands of the clock tower causing it to jam. In 1989 the Royal Marines Band finally left and transferred to HMS *Nelson* in Queen Street, taking two of the old Crimean mortars with them as souvenirs, and renaming their new accommodation 'Eastney Block'. They returned two years later to play out the last Royal Marines to leave on the 31st October 1991; the final detachment being led through the gates by the late Captain Ken Gill RM.

Former naval married quarters and the 'Centurion Gate' housing development share the site of the Sea Service Gunnery School, 2008.

View from Eastney Fort East over the playing fields towards the former 1950s' married quarters of Halliday Crescent. They were vacated and boarded up in 2008.

Farewell to Eastney Although the Royal Marines had taken over Eastney Barracks with little pomp or ceremony, this was not the case when they departed. The final series of seasonal concerts in St Andrew's Church was a sell-out with the Principal Director of Music, Royal Marines, a) here seen at rehearsal, conducting the final one. b) Afterwards, members of the band continued the entertainment. c) The band combined with the Museum to stage a 'Farewell to Eastney' concert evening and, d) also took part, with the Kings Squad and other representatives of the Corps, in a ceremonial display in the Guildhall Square – in pouring rain. On the day of the march-out e) the last RM Detachment, commanded by Captain K Gill RM formally handed over the 'Keys of Eastney'; the Union flag was lowered and f) the band marched out the Detachment for the very last time.

d)

e)

f)

11 Eastney from 1990

Sculpted in resin and bronze by Philip Jackson, the 18 foot Royal Marine 'Yomper' was unveiled by the former Prime Minister Margaret Thatcher on 8th July 1992. The statue was based on the photograph of Corporal Peter Robinson RM marching to Sapper Hill after the cease fire in the 1982 Falklands War. The figure is of no one particular Royal Marine, and many of the details including the captured Argentine High Combat Boots being worn, come from a number of different images.

THE MINISTRY OF DEFENCE announced in early 1990 that they intended to dispose of the Eastney Barracks site. The area of the site released extended to approximately 30 acres and included the main barrack block and land to the south, Eastney Fort West and land to the south and west of the Parade Ground. Also included was the area to the north of the Museum including St Andrew's Church, which had merged its designation with the Parish of St James Church in Milton since 1973. The existing Royal Marines Museum and Eastney Fort East were retained from the sale, along with the playing fields.

A Planning Brief for the Royal Marines Barracks was approved by Portsmouth City Council on 4 December 1990 and the site was auctioned in spring 1992. The whole site was bought by property developers, Gudgeon Homes who set about conversion works to some of the buildings. They then sold their ownership interest in the land to Redrow Homes (South East) Ltd in June 1995 and part of the land adjacent to St Andrew's Church, off Henderson Road, to Southlands Housing Association.

The barracks site included Scheduled Ancient Monuments, Listed Buildings, and was itself an unusual conservation area because the centrepiece was not so much the buildings but the relationship of the buildings to the open Parade Ground. Eastney Fort East and West and the connecting bank were Scheduled Ancient Monuments, as was the boundary wall surrounding the site. The Officers' Mess (which included the Royal Marines Museum), main barrack block, officers' quarters and water tower (or clock tower) were all Grade II listed buildings.

The group of buildings between the western end of the main barrack block and the clock tower were not listed as at December 1990, but were nevertheless important visually in forming a sense of enclosure to this corner of the Parade Ground. However the Impress Building, which had been last used by the Civilian Administration Officer, the PSA, and the Special Investigations Branch, was demolished.

Aerial view of the main barracks' gate in Cromwell Road, showing the rear of 'Teapot Row' behind the clock tower.

The Officers' Mess dining room was renamed the 'Mountbatten Dining Room' by the RM Museum and is here arranged for a wedding banquet.

The RM Museum originally had a commemorative rose garden in front of the Officers' Mess stairs with the Lumsden memorial as a centre piece. After the selling and conversion to housing of St Andrew's Church, earth and ashes from both gardens were incorporated into the new Memorial Garden shown here.

In July 1991 planning permission was granted to use the north wing of the Officers' Mess as a Museum extension and form a car park adjacent to the Museum, in front of the bank. Work started on site in October 1995.

In January 1994 permission was granted for the construction of a 5-6 storey building with alterations and conversion of Nos. 11-14 Eastney Terrace, the clock tower and adjacent buildings to form fifty-six self-contained apartments along with associated landscaping, roads and car parking. These works were started in March 1994 and completed in July 1995.

A month later in February 1994 further applications were passed for alterations to the main barrack blocks to form forty-two self-contained flats and the construction of seventy 2-3 storey 2 and 3 bedroom dwellings with associated garages, roads and landscaping on land between the north of the barrack block and Lidiard Gardens. Work commenced in October 1994 and completed in June 1996.

The minstrels' gallery of the RM Museum as it appears in July 2008.

At the same time (February 1994) agreement was reached for sixty-one 2-storey houses and two 2-storey blocks comprising twenty-three flats along with associated roads, car parking and landscaping on land south east of Lidiard Gardens and south of Henderson Road.

The scheme also included conversion of the former St Andrew's Church to form a community centre, but this was abandoned in favour of converting it into nine dwellings. The rose garden by the church had long been used for the scattering of ashes, so the RM Museum excavated the beds and used the soil to make a Memorial Garden along the northern edge of its lawns. The Museum also removed any memorial plaques and fittings from the church before the conversion took place; those unable to be separated from the fabric of the building were boarded over and recorded so that they can be considered at any future date when the building may be changed or altered.

In May 1994, an additional ten dwellings were added to this scheme and in August a further two were added.

The Main Parade in 2008 with the additional 'Parade View Mansions' built in 1997.

By October 1994 permission was granted for the conversion of the former officers' quarters to form fourteen apartments and a hotel along with seven 2-3 storey houses north of the adjacent Eastney Fort West. This scheme was revised in February 1995 to form sixteen apartments and a hotel, and then modified in April with the dropping of the hotel element. Works had begun on converting the building in November 1994.

In August 1999 work was finally completed on the construction of a four-storey building to form twenty flats, with associated parking and landscaping; this was called 'Parade View Mansions'. 'The Clock Tower', 'The Armoury', 'The Drill House', and 'The Colonnades' were Phase 2 conversion developments by Redrow. 'The Gate House' was another new building constructed on the old, demolished, Motor Transport Section garages, consisting of six apartments. This whole area was named 'Marine Gate'.

It was a condition of the planning consent for 'The Clock Tower' that all four dials should be made operational. Redrow and their subcontractor, Warings Ltd trusted the work to Stephen Philips of Aylsham, who utilised the existing hands, dial and motion-work, and fitted individual heavy duty electric drive motors interlinked with a synchroniser unit and battery back-up system. The four dials were restored in situ, in often difficult climatic conditions. Applying twenty-three and a quarter carat gold leaf at this exposed site is a tribute to the dial restorer.

This electrical clock system was put into use in the summer of 1997, with inaugural start-up ceremony at the end of July attended by many 'notables' involved with this prestigious project, including Colonel Keith Wilkins RM, the then Director of the Royal Marines Museum.

'Gunners Walk' was divided into seven houses of six apartments over three floors, named after seven of the Royal Marines Victoria Cross winners. Parker, Lumsden, and Hunter were not used, and strangely were not selected for any of the new building names or roads. Redrow had already decided on 'Churchill Square' and 'Mountbatten Square' when they contacted the Museum Archivist for other appropriate names for the development's roads. Of those suggested, the remaining Victoria Cross recipients were not used, but Pitcairn, Hopkins, Saunders, Drysdale and Flinders were. Flinders was a Royal Navy Captain who took a Marine detachment to chart southern Australia in 1801-3, but was not top of the list when submitted.

Seen from the sea the 'Gunners Walk' apartments were simply named left to right in alphabetical order rather than the date of the Victoria Cross being awarded, or relevance to the barracks. Lumsden, who served in the RMA was left off, but the presence of his memorial in the Museum grounds may have been the reason.

- A block became Bamford House
- B block became Dowell House
- C block became Finch House
- D block became Halliday House
- E block became Harvey House
- F block became Prettyjohns House
- G block became Wilkinson House

The completion of most of the conversions came at a time when the housing market was in decline and the pricing for the prestigious flats was under severe pressure. The ground floor show flat in Gunners Walk that was formally the RM Museums' store for display cases and canoes was priced at £80000, while a top floor apartment was to be £125000 in 1994. Those customers with the means to afford these prices at this time made one of the best property investments of the decade as the market went on to recover into the next century.

12 Eastney's Musical Accompaniment

MUSIC, whether from marching band, orchestra or the sound of bugle calls or the beating of drums, has always been associated with the Royal Marines. This could be through entertainment for the officers and other ranks, for the local population or through the means of broadcast or recordings. For many, the mere mention of 'Royal Marines' conjures a mental image of a Bugler, a Drum Major or a band. Valid though these examples of their ceremonial and entertainment value might be, they are not the real reason, even reasons, for their inception or continued existence. Military bands, of all shape, size and type, were once likened to 'the first military transport department' since their role was to move men about – not by carrying them but by leading them at a constant pace with rousing, heartening music. By simple extension they could also be likened to 'the first military signals department' since the original role of the Drummer, later Bugler in the case of the Royal Marines, was to transfer orders and instructions from officers to men under their command.

The RMA, drawn up in marching order and fronted by their Divisional Band, prepare to march to Southsea Common for an Inspection in May 1868. Based upon the date and place it is believed that the man to the right of the band, not carrying an instrument, is Bandmaster Thomas Smyth.

RMA Band marching men back from the Fort Cumberland training areas towards Eastney Barracks. The hummock, centre background, in the fork of the road, is believed to be the site of the old Point Battery. (see map below).

This map of Eastney Village and the early musketry field quite clearly shows a bandstand. This must have been used by the Royal Marine Artillery Band whilst it was stationed in Fort Cumberland between 1861 and approximately 1868.

When the Band of the Royal Marine Artillery marched a detachment from Chatham and Woolwich Division into the barracks, Thomas Smyth was the Bandmaster and the band consisted of forty-six Musicians and eight Boy Musicians. The band had been formed in 1861, at Fort Cumberland, by Colonel John Fraser. The official march past was Gounod's 'The Soldier's Chorus' from *Faust* and this would remain the case until the official adoption of *A Life on the Ocean Wave* in 1882. A number of good bandmasters maintained the high standard of the band such that, at the turn of the twentieth century, it was well-established in a large, well-equipped barracks and with a very competent Bandmaster, B S Green.

As the men of the RMA moved into Fort Cumberland and then Eastney Barracks so the sound of the ever present Buglers was heard. These men, collectively known as either the Corps of Drums or Drums and Bugles Company, were a large group of men and boys who had enlisted to be trained to play bugle, drum and, in some cases, fife, for the purposes of signalling, marching groups of men when no band was available or ceremonial and entertainment. At a certain age they would either transfer to become a 'general' marine or could stay as a Bugler. These men were administered by a Bugler Major. Buglers were, by comparison with today, a very large component of the Division. Every ship's RM Detachment would have

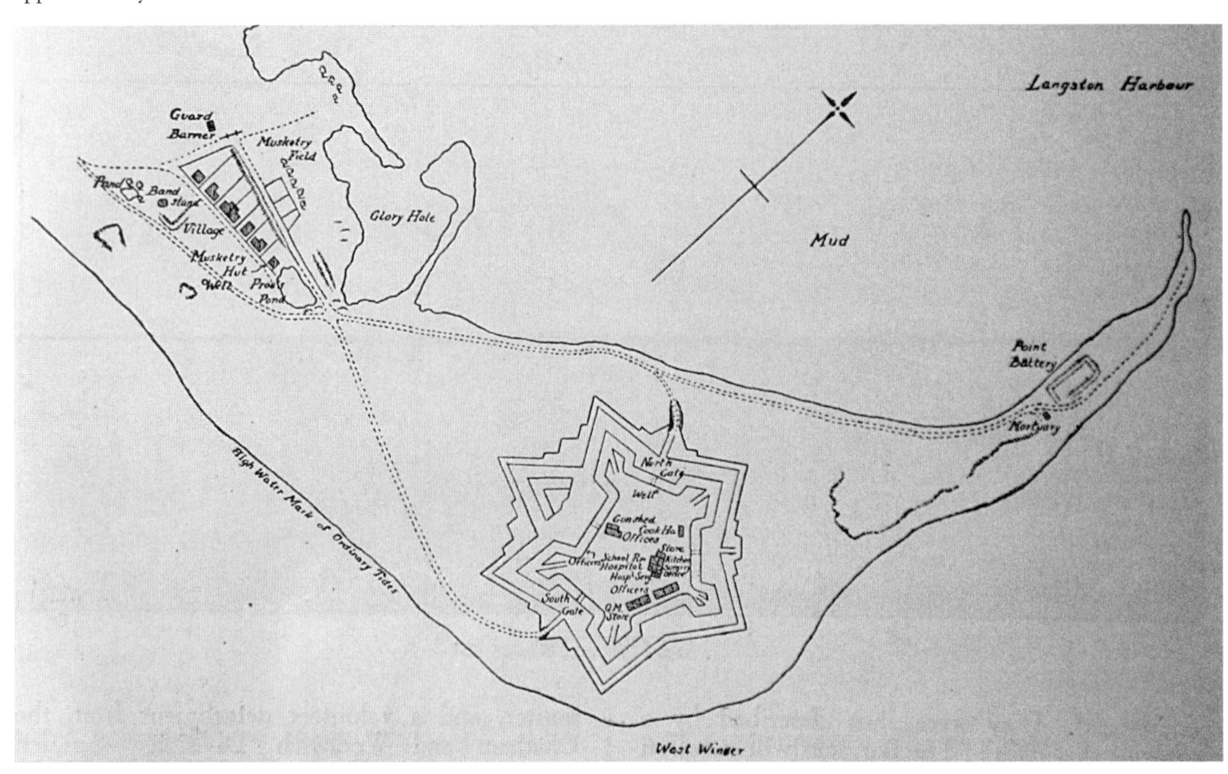

at least two, they would be required for duty in all establishments and a number of them would accompany practically every party of Marines on exercise or training. For major ceremonial the Buglers would join with the RMA Band, very often in enough numbers to provide a Corps of Drums at the head of the band with ranks of men playing bugles or fifes at the rear.

An additional, and unique, organization joined the barracks in 1903. It had been decided that the Royal Marines would become responsible for all the musical requirements of the Royal Navy through a Royal Naval School of Music located at Eastney and administered, in the main, by the Royal Marine Artillery. This was to be an organization distinct from the RMA Divisional Band and would train and prepare bands for all of the Royal Navy's ships and shore establishments in the same way that the Divisions supplied RMA/RMLI Detachments and Buglers. In addition to their musical training they were given a military role and were trained in ship's gunnery communications. Later this would be expanded to the skilled work of operating the ship's transmitting stations. These were located in the bowels of the ship, were difficult to escape from and led to a very high percentage casualty rate in both World Wars. This situation continued until 1930 when the school, desperately needing more space for training the numbers of musicians needed by the Royal Navy, was relocated to Deal, Kent.

At the time of the amalgamation the Royal Marine Artillery Band became the Royal Marines Portsmouth Division Band, a title that was altered from Division to Group in 1950 when the amalgamation of the Royal Marines Divisional Bands with the Royal Naval School of Music,

Captain B S Green, Director of Music Royal Marine Artillery, 6th November 1919. Signed two years after he retired.

The Drums of the Royal Marine Artillery 1919. The two men in the centre are Brig Gen G M Campbell and the Adjutant, Captain A L Forster DSO. The Bugle Major sits on the Brigadier's right whilst the Drum Major is seated to the Adjutant's left. Although difficult to see, the Drum Major is wearing the special cap badge given to the RMA Band by King George V in 1911. He wears this because he is technically part of the band although he would also monitor the progress of the Buglers. He carries his short staff, the full staff being laid across the drums.

The cornet and baritone class of the Royal Naval School of Music, Eastney, in October 1905. Professor E Wakeford, who would have been the instrument professor at the school at that time, is the civilian.

took place. During the rationalization of the 1970s they became the Band of the Royal Marines, C-in-C Naval Home Command, a title they held until the closure of Eastney and the march-out of October 1991.

In 1903 the King had gazetted the Royal Marine Artillery Band as the permanent Royal Yacht Band, an honour that was handed on to the various bands that succeeded them until HMY *Britannia* was decommissioned in 1997. At that time HM The Queen officially gave the Royal Marines Portsmouth Band the additional title of 'The Royal Band'.

A group of Band Boys from the RN School of Music doing Swedish Drill in the Eastney gymnasium 1911.

Men of the Royal Naval School of Music Parade for the Adjutant General's inspection, 1909. This is the small parade outside the school, not the main Barracks Parade.

General LST Halliday VC, Adjutant General RM, inspecting ranks of the RN School of Music at Eastney c.1927.

The Royal Marine Band sent by the Royal Naval School of Music to serve at Admiralty House, Queenstown, Ireland, in 1910. They are seen about to perform as an orchestra. Just like the Divisional Bands, the Royal Naval School of Music trained men to play orchestral as well as military band instruments. Although they wear the Corps cap badge the men of the RNSM can be differentiated by the lyre collar badge that they wore.

The Band of the Royal Marines, Portsmouth, (The Royal Band) give a concert and Beat Retreat annually at the Royal Marines Museum. Here, the finale of the 2002 Beat Retreat takes place on the grass outside the Museum and Gunners Walk.

Bibliography, sources, and further reading

John Ambler *The Royal Marines Band Service* (Royal Marines Historical Society SP28:2003).

Richard Brooks *The Royal Marines 1664 to the present* (Constable, 2002)

General Sir HE Blumberg KCB RM: *Britain's Sea Soldiers – A Record of the Royal Marines During the War 1914-1919* (Swiss, Devonport 1927, reprinted Naval and Military Press, Uckfield 2007)

Colonal Cyril Field RMLI *Britain's Sea Soldiers* vols i & ii (Lyceum Press, Liverpool 1924)

E Fraser & LG Carr Laughton *The Royal Marine Artillery* (RUSI 1930) vols i & ii

James Douet *British Barracks 1600-1914* (English Heritage 1998)

The Globe & Laurel (The journal of the Royal Marines 1892 to present)

Captain G W M Grover RM *History of the Royal Marine Divisions* (Globe & Laurel, Eastney 1931)

Colonel I S Harrison RM *Royal Marine Barracks Eastney – Arrival Information Handbook* (Littlebury & Co. Worcester, 1966)

English Heritage *A guide to the history and selected buildings of Fort Cumberland* (2004)

Alexander N Y Howell *Notes on the Topology of Portsmouth* (W H Barrell, Portsmouth 1913)

Colonel H James RE *Plans of the Barracks in the South Western District of England* (War Office, 1859)

James D Ladd *By Sea, By Land – The Royal Marines 1919-1997* (Harper Collins 1998)

Andrew Lane *The Royal Marines Barracks, Eastney* (Halsgrove Tiverton 1998)

Sharon Lee & John Steadman *Voices from Eastney – a spoken history* (Portsmouth City Council, 2003)

M G Little: *The Royal Marines and the Victoria Cross* (Royal Marines Museum, Eastney, 2002)

The London Illustrated News (1890)

JA Lowe *Records of the Portsmouth Division of Marines* 1764-1800 (City of Portsmouth 1990)

Philip A Magrath *Fort Cumberland 1747-1850 Key to an Island's Defence* (Portsmouth City Council, 1992)

Public Catalogue Foundation *Oil Paintings in Public Ownership on Hampshire.* (Public Catalogue Foundation, 2007)

David Moore *Eastney Battery East* (Palmeston Forts Society, 2002)

The Portsmouth News (1958)

WEA *Memories of Eastney* (WEA Portsmouth Branch Local History Group, 1994)

Archive Sources

Extensive use has been made of the Royal Marines Museum Archive in the writing of this book. The principal document collections for further research are:

Arch 2/7/6 The Royal Marine Artillery (Division) 1804 – 1923

Arch 16/9/3 The Divisional Schools

Arch 17/2/5 Eastney Barracks

Arch 17/5/2 Fort Cumberland

Arch 17/6/2 The Crinoline Church and St Andrew's Church

Index

Subscribers' List

Colonel Charles Ackroyd TD RD, Southsea, Hampshire
Mr Ivan Allen, Walsall
R.J. Allen, Portsmouth
Keith Anderson 2008
Phillip Archer, Macclesfield, Cheshire
RM9325 S. L. Arnold, 40 Commando
C.L. Asher, Ex C/SGT, Dunfermline
Frank E. G. Attrill, Bourton, Dorset
Arthur E. Awcock, 432 SQUAD, Canvey Island, Essex
Keith Babington, Blairgowrie, Perthshire
John W. Baker, RM 13575, Enfield, Middlesex
Tom Baker-Cresswell, Northumberland
Major J.C. Barden, RM
Mr Andrew C. Barnes, Downham Market, Norfolk
Gordon Bealby, Beckenham, Kent
Ken Bean, Formby, Ex (RM 130492)
Mr John D. Beare, Plymouth
W.B. Bell, former C/SGT RM, East Yorkshire
Harold B. Berry, FRTPI, Liskeard, Cornwall
Thomas I. Bevan, Eltham, London
Norman W. Bickley, Solihull
F. L. Blackman, Brynmawr, Blaenau, Gwent
David Blackmore, Portsmouth, Hampshire
Mr Graham Bland, Polegate, East Sussex
Frank Bolton, Liskeard, Cornwall
Kenneth Booth, Worcester
Ian Booth, Isle of Man
Colin Bowden, Malvern, Worcs
Ex Marine G. Bowers, Deal
B. Boyce, West Midlands
The Rev'd Albert Braithwaite R.N., Southsea
Robert C. Briscoe, Shrewsbury, Shropshire
Donald S. Broad, North Norfolk
Fergus J.M. Brown, WS, Peebles
William J. Bryan, Deal
Rick and Eileen Bucksey (Sgt RM Ret'd), Perth, Western Australia
Ann Burrows, Beverley, Yorks. Dedicated to the memory of ex-Marine Ernest F., Burrows, POX 5733, 1946-1964.
John W. Busby, Milton-under-Wychwood
Ian Campbell, Marine (D), Eastney Transport 1967 - 1970
Colonel J.D.F.H. Cantrell, Trowbridge, Wilts
Kenneth J. Carpenter, Poole
Colonel Brian L. Carter OBE RM, Gosport, Hants
George S. Chandler, Rowlands Castle, Hants
Graham E. Chapman, Perth, Western Australia
Lt Col M. J. Chilcott, Normandy, France
Raymond Clausen, RM127932, 982 Squad, Chatham, 1948-1950
Mr and Mrs E. Cole, Whitstable, Kent
Pat Collins, Bedhampton, Hants
QMS RM PO/X5204 John Cook, South Australia
Henry Cooper, Dunkeswell
Harry Corben, U4 Squad, 42 Commando,
T.W.M. Cotter (former Royal Marine, RM8879), Eltham, London
Mark H. Couchman, Lenham, Kent
William Joseph Coughlan, Portsmouth, Hants
William J. W. Courtenay CBE, Weybridge, Surrey
RM 11332 Jock Cowan 1951/74, CLR/Sgt HM Ships Kenya, Ceylon, Vanguard, Bellerophon,
Victorious, Intrepid. CDO's 40, 42 & 43
Ernie Crisp, CHX107497, Southend on Sea
CTCRM Lympstone, Corps Library
Daphne M. H. Daniels, Petersfield
Victor G. Day JP, Shrivenham, Oxon
Ken Denniss, Cleethorpes, Lincs
R. Derbyshire, RM20612 MNE (D), Accrington, Lancs
Brian Dexter, Mattishall, Norfolk
Mr H. Dodds, Southampton
Major A.J. Donald R.M, Horndean, Hants
Kenneth Dorans, RM
Peter G. Downs
Lt Col E. J. Eagles RM
Geoff Eames, Ex RM
C. N. Elliott EX2845, Skelmersdale, Lancs
Dennis "Lofty" Emerton, Australia
Mr Joe Fairclough, Plymouth
Christopher F. W. Fairey MBE, Plymouth, Devon
Norman Feather, Leeds, Yorks
Mr Ken Fields, Southend-on-Sea
Patricia M. Finn, Plymouth
Geoffrey Fletcher, Belgium
Jack D. Fletcher, Caton, Lancaster
Peter J. Foot, Orba, Alicante
Mr J. A. Forster, Gateshead, Tyne and Wear
Mr J. A. Forster, Poole, Dorset
Margaret E. Frimley, Plymouth
Dennis Fullwood, London
RQMS T. Gentry, To my Husband, love Kate
Alan Gibson, Malaga, Spain
Roy Gillett, Alverstoke
Marine H. Goldman, Leeds, Yorks
Captain Paul Goodlet RM, Thorncombe, Chard, Somerset
John Gordon, 631 Squad Royal Marines
Roland Graham RM 24427, Carlisle, Cumbria
Dr and Mrs Ivor Grayson-Smith, Southsea
T.W. Grieves BEM. (EX C/SGT DI and CA), Hartlepool
MNE Griffiths RM 18465, Wirral, Cheshire

Mr Anthony R. Hacker, Wilton, Wiltshire
Leslie R. Harley, Former PO/X 5791, Risca, Gwent
John Peter Harpham, Royal Marine CHX 115836
'Cabby' Harris, Atp 45RM CDO (Vintage), Wickford, Essex
Edward A. Hartley, Long Buckby
Frank Harwood
Peter Hasting
Major A.J. Hawley RM, Curry Rivel
Kathy Heine, Walmer
David and Susan Hewett, Gunners Row, Southsea
David W. Hollyoak, Oldbury, West Midlands
Stephen R. Houghton, Herefordshire
Mr Peter Eric Howse, Gosport
Christopher J. R. Hunt, London
David Hurl RM, Fareham, Hants
Colin Ireland, Baker Troop
Andy R. D. Jackson MBE, Fareham, Hampshire
R.A. Jarrett R.M. 7740, Waltham Cross, Hertfordshire
Trefor and Joan Jones, Burgh Heath, Surrey
Mr R. T. Jones, New Ferry, Wirral
Brian E Joyles, Croydon, Surrey
T.A. Judge B.E.M., Cheshire
Mr Rip Kirby, Hull
Ronald J. Knight, Bury St Edmunds, Suffolk
Ken "Bogie" Knight, Edmonton, London
Mr Michael Korrie, New Milton, Hampshire
Ken Large, Middleton St. George
G.T. Lawrence, Canvey Island, Essex
Reginald A. Leach, Cliftonville, Kent
Mr Barry J. Lee, Banwell, Somerset
Kenneth R.J. Legg, Swanage, Dorset
Harry Lewis, Caerphilly, Glamorgan
Mr David C.E. Lewry, Gosport, Hants
B.S. Libby, Torpoint, Cornwall
Captain Albert Lilley, West Kirby, Wirral
Phoebe and Emma Little, Rowlands Castle, Hampshire
Fred Lunn, Leigh, Lancashire
Roy William Lunn, RM 8066, Bristol
Robert Mackintosh, Plymtree, Devon
F.C. Mackrell, 40 and 45 Commando, 1964 - 1974, Worthing, West Sussex
Ian Maine
D. Marshall, FLT LT RAF (RETD)
Mr William Martin, Carlisle, Cumbria
William F. Maundrell, Maidenhead, Berks
PO/X6669 C/Sgt G. R. McCarroll RM (Rtd)
Finlay McCulloch, St Columb Major
Alan McGregor, Tywyn, Wales
Mne John Graham McKelvie, RMV203009 NS 921 Sqad Oct 1957-59
Mr Horace E. Mendham, RSM, Portsmouth
Jenny and Tony Mendoza, Portsmouth
LCPL Justin M. Montague, Swindon
Anthony W. Moore (RM 9649), Hinckley, Leics
Kevin A. Morris J.P.
Ken Mumford, RM 10268, R.M.A. Norfolk
Dave Mustow, Jersey, C.I.
William H. Nellist, Macclesfield, Cheshire
Lt Col Paul Neville
John F. Newnham MBE, Royal Marines Association, Shrewsbury, Shropshire
Robert Charles Niddrie, Morestead, Winchester
Leonard E. North, St Albans, Herts
Ellen North, Loughborough, Leicestershire,
Captain Derek A. Oakley MBE RM, Hayling Island, Hants
Peter Osborne, RM9258 Chatham
Mr Martin Paul Osborne, Bradwell, Norfolk
Keith W.E. Osborne MBE, Yealmpton, Devon
H.D. Overbury, Exmouth, Devon
Theo Palmer, Woodhall Spa, LN10 6QU
Mr George A. Pearson, Coventry, Warwickshire
R.G. Pennell, EX JE19, Tavistock
Anthony J. Perrett, Gosport
Major Bob Perry RM, Navy Command Headquarters, Portsmouth
Ken Phillips, 42 Commando Royal Marines
Mark Phillips, Sanjose, California
Donald Pimp, MNE RM 7690, Harrogate
Francis E. Pocock, Thatcham, Berkshire
Eric David Pointer
Reginald J. Pope, Plymouth, Devon
Ex PLY/X5364 QMS J.A. Porter, Deal, Kent
Edward Postin, 12949, Warwickshire
Geoffrey R. Potten - Grandfather of Marine David J. Pink (KB) PO65085G,
Christopher T. Powe, Plymouth, Devon
David Powell, Captain Royal Marines (Rtd)
Charles (Sandy) Powell, Waterlooville, Hants
Mr and Mrs J.W. Powell, Bedhampton, Havant, Hampshire
Mr Rodney Preston, Portsmouth, Hants
David Prichard
Alfred J. Pugh, PLYX5485 481 SQUAD, Birmingham
Mr John Rawling, Clevedon
Fred W. Rayers, Malvern
Dennis E. Read, Borehamwood, Herts
E. Redstone, Portsmouth
Dennis Reynolds, Gresford
Geoffrey Richards, Hilperton
Fredrick Rigby, Plymouth, Devon
Major R.T.F. Rigden MBE RM,
Major Ernest A. Rigsby RM, Catherington
Andrew E. Rigsby RM, Lane End
Adrian P. Rigsby RM, Taunton
M.D. Roberts, RM24158 MNE
C. N. Robinson, Fishbourne, Chichester
Royal Marines Corps Secretariat
Mr Mike Saloway EX 862 N/S Squad, New Milton
Geoffrey and Madeleine Salvetti, Eastney, Hampshire
"Fritz" Salzmann, Aldermaston. Berks

Keith Sanders, Poole
George Sankey, Whitechurch, Hants
Captain John E. Sargent RM, Wimborne, Dorset
M.D. Savage, Dover
Bob Saynor, Leeds, Yorkshire
Tom Scade, Dunfermline, Fife
D. J. Scott RM 128777 MNE 1950-1952 N.S.
Wilfred R. Severn, Oldbury, West Midlands
P.C. Shapter, 977 Squad, Plymouth, Devon
John W. Sharpe, Deal
Mrs F.J. Sharpe, Southsea, Hants
Stephan G. Sheppard, Spalding
Colonel R. C. Sidwell, Sidmouth, Devon
Roy W. Sim, Birkenhead
Evan Simpson, Chester-le-Street, Co Durham
J. Smee, RM 8633 541 SQUAD
Mr Peter Smith, Hull, Yorkshire
Bryan Smith, Salisbury, South Australia
Mike Smith, Gillette, N.J.
Robert A.S. Smith, Bournville, Birmingham
W.I. Smith, 586 Squad, Chesham, Bucks
Allan J. Spain, Former Chatham Marine
William H. Stanton, Romford
Mr J Stephens, Gosport
Captain John S. Stewart OBE FRAgS RM (Retd)
Graham H. Stokes, Deal, Kent
Pam and Keith Stoneman FRMM,
Roger G. Stonestreet, Lee-on-the-Solent
Michael M. Tanner, Ferring, Sussex
Frank Taylor, PLY/X4780, Swansea
Major Norman Thackeray, Hopton Castle, Shropshire
Paul Thistlewood, Thorness, Isle of Wight
Hilary Thomas, Southsea, Hants
David J. Thorp, Plymouth
Jack Townley, Kings Lynn, Norfolk
Mike and Jenny Trotman, Eastney Church, 14.09.68
Major P.B. Troy, RM, Jersey
Martin and Christine Tuppen, Formby, Merseyside
John Venner, Sydney, Australia
Gerald Victor (Vic) Rogers, 45 Commando, Andover, Hants
Peter W. Waight, Eastney
Alan W. Waite, 641 CS Squad
Joe Wall (PO/X6215), Halesowen, West Mids
L.J. Walters, Ex SGT. GI., Peterborough, Cambs
Major E. H. Warren MBE RM, Dorset
Captain S. G. G. Weall, Royal Marines
Jonathan David Henry Weller
R.F. West,
K. West, Winchester
Lt Col J. C. Weston MC RM (Rtd),
Peter J. Westwood, New Malden, Surey
Valerie Whaley, East Dean, Eastbourne
Ken Whiterod, Bexley, Kent
Doreen Wilce, Havant, Hants
Christopher J. Wilkinson, Peel, Isle of Man
Ross M.A. Wilson, F.C.M.H, RM Historical Society
Peter and Cheryl Wingett, Historical Diving Society
Dave Wood, Jersey, C.I.
E.A. Wright, PO/X6181, Isleworth
Peter L.E. Wye, PLY/X117156 (976 Squad), Clacton On Sea, Essex
Kenneth J. York RM 1937 - 1960 POX4691 QMS, York